Dawlish Sea Wall
The Railway between Exeter and Newton Abbot

Colin J. Marsden

Ian Allan
PUBLISHING

CONTENTS

ACKNOWLEDGEMENTS

The Author would like to thank the many people who have contributed directly and indirectly to the production of this title. A special thank you is due to the number of photographers who have allowed me access to their valuable photographic collections, especially Mr Brian Stephenson who made available his entire Rail Archive Stephenson collection of images recorded on the Dawlish and Teignmouth Sea Wall section, allowing a number of century-old images to be seen for the first time.

Many local people from Dawlish and the surrounding area have assisted with personal memories and recollections as well as early pictures of rail operations, and to these people I am indebted.

A special thank you also goes to a number of retired and serving railway staff who have answered countless, often trivial questions about the local area and its rail operation.

Finally I would like to thank my family and friends, especially Mrs Jean Marsden, Miss Wendy Etheridge, Mr Keith Ewing, Mr Andy Gay, Mr Kevin Wills, Mr Nathan Williamson and lastly but most importantly Miss Nicky Hill and Mr John Grindrod, the proprietors of The Laffinn Pig public house in Dawlish, for providing much welcome liquid refreshment during the evenings and an excellent meeting house at which to talk about railways.

Title Page: *Great Western 3521 class 4-4-0 No. 3547 awaits the right away from Dawlish with an up stopping service in 1926. This loco had an eventful life; it was built as an 0-4-2ST to broad gauge specification in 1888, but due to unsteady running when converted to standard gauge, it was rebuilt as an 0-4-4T in 1891. Although more successful, the design was still unstable and between 1899-1902 all 40 of the class were again rebuilt as 4-4-0 tender locomotives.* **Bernard Whicher/Rail Archive Stephenson**

Front Cover: *Viewed from Lea Mount and looking over the Dawlish Sea Wall towards Exmouth and east Devon, Freightliner Heavy Haul Class 66/6 No. 66620 passes Dawlish station on 30 August 2007 powering train 6Z60, the 10.51 Neasden to Newton Abbot Hackney yard. The train is formed of empty sand hoppers bound for Burngullow, which after loading operated to Angerstein Wharf in north Kent.* **Author**

Rear Cover Top: *Taken in the spring of 1926, Great Western 'Saint' class 4-6-0 No. 2977 Robertson approaches the Rockstone Bridge mid way between Dawlish and Dawlish Warren, powering a Plymouth to Liverpool cross-country express.* **Bernard Whicher/Rail Archive Stephenson**

Rear Cover Bottom: *Heading towards Kennaway Tunnel on the Dawlish Sea Wall, BR Swindon-built 'Warship' diesel-hydraulic No. D800 Sir Brian Robertson passes through a rough sea on 17 September 1960 powering the 'Royal Duchy' service from London Paddington to Penzance.* **Peter Gray**

First published 2009

ISBN 978 0 7110 3374 0

Published by Ian Allan Publishing Ltd, Hersham, Surrey KT12 4RG.

Printed in England by Ian Allan Ltd, Hersham, Surrey KT12 4RG.

Code: 0904/B2

Visit the Ian Allan Publishing website at www.ianallanpublishing.com

Above: *The classic view of Dawlish Sea Wall, viewed from Lea Mount, looking towards the station, with the coast-edge footpath between the sea and railway. On 21 September 2008, a five vehicle train of autoballaster wagons top and tailed by EWS Class 66s Nos. 66005 and 66040 head west towards Kennaway Tunnel forming an Exeter Riverside Yard to Long Rock ballast train.* **Author**

INTRODUCTION

Firstly, welcome to *Dawlish Sea Wall: The Railway between Exeter and Newton Abbot*. Over the years much has been written about the 21 miles of railway line between Exeter and Aller, West of Newton Abbot which is affectionately knows as The Dawlish Sea Wall line.

There is probably no other section of railway line in the world which attracts the interest that the Dawlish Sea Wall generates. Locations such as Dawlish, Langstone Rock and Cockwood Harbour are without doubt the most photographed locations anywhere, with on some occasions when special or unusual locomotives have passed by, upwards of 200 photographers being recorded.

There are likely to be many reasons why the route has attracted such interest – its splendid scenery, ease of access and wide variety of train types are the most common reasons, but the not infrequent inclement weather with waves crashing over the line inflicting structural damage to the fabric of the line also attracts interest, especially if people can stand and watch the storm seas crashing over the line and into the streets.

The national media has also done its part in highlighting the area with frequent, often sarcastic, comments about delays to trains on the Sea Wall due to rough seas, boats on the line and the infamous problems at the start of this century of Virgin Voyager trains just stopping in rough weather, stranding passengers on the open section of the Sea Wall.

Over 20 years ago I had the pleasure of moving from the leafy suburbs of Surrey to Dawlish. One of the things which attracted me to the area was, of course, the railway and its diversity of operations, and still today without major difficulty a wide variety of trains can still be observed and photographed. Another reason for my move to Dawlish was the very pleasant people who live in the area; it is a much slower way of life than the London commuter belt and generally a much more pleasing environment in which to live.

This title has been put together to try and show in pictures and words the changing scene of the railways of Dawlish over the years. I have included several views of the same location in some instances, to show railway changes as well as developments and changes in the townscapes and buildings. Towns such as Dawlish have grown hugely over the years and just a quick review of pictures taken from the ever popular Lea Mount on the west side of the town reveals some significant changes to the landscape.

While the contour of the railway has changed little in the last 100 years the rock faces in both Dawlish and Teignmouth and especially around Parsons Head have changed quite dramatically with erosion of the soft sandstone.

I hope that the readers and viewers of this title obtain as much pleasure from browsing its pages as it has given me in putting it all together and writing the captions.

Colin J Marsden
Dawlish, March 2009

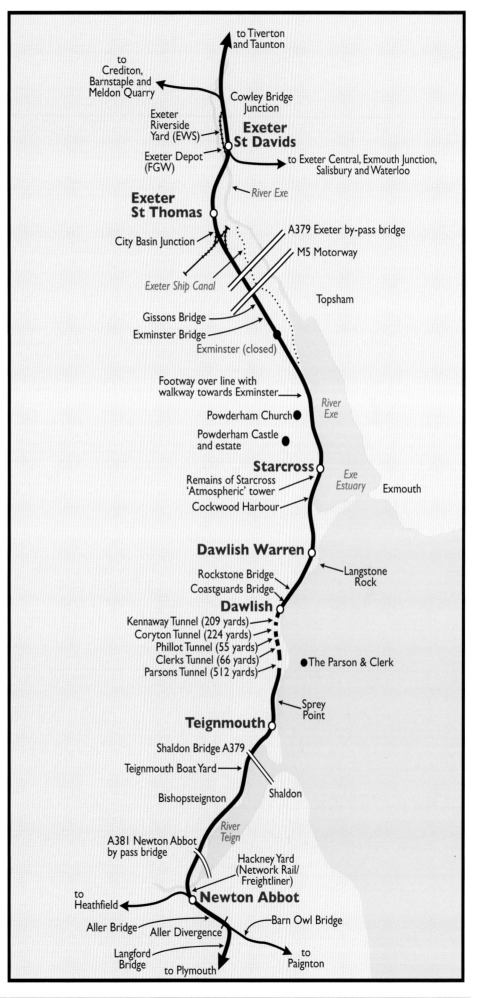

Proof of a settlement in Dawlish did not come until 1044 when King Edward the Confessor, the last Anglo-Saxon king of England, granted the parish of Dawlish to his then Chancellor and chaplain, Leofric, on the condition that he built bridges and supplied soldiers to construct defences in time of war.

The charter explaining this donation is kept in the archives of Exeter Cathedral and is well preserved. Much of it was written in Latin, although the boundaries of the land donated were given in English (Anglo-Saxon). This is the oldest record of Dawlish in history. However, it is quite possible that a community existed centuries before, even back to the period of the Saxon invasions in the 5th and 6th centuries AD, as the parish church of Dawlish was dedicated to St. Gregory the Great.

When Leofric arrived, the manor of Dawlish extended from roughly Teignmouth in the south to Cofton and Cockwood in the north, and the top of Haldon Hill in the west. It was a large area, mostly uninhabited and covered in thick forest, as it would have been difficult to cultivate with poor soil.

The main reason that settlers established a 'village' in the area was that it was protected, sheltered on three sides by hills and on the remaining face by the sea. The presence of the sea provided limited food, while the wooded area harboured animals which gave meat, and wood for burning to give heating and a method of cooking, as well as for building. The presence of several fresh water rivers gave drinkable water. Work was provided by cultivating salt marshes which also gave a method of preserving food but above all gave trade with other communities.

At this time the settlement which grew into Dawlish was not on the coast, the sea was feared by most, nobody knew what was 'over the water's edge', it was known by locals that damaging storms emerged from the sea which also flooded the land, so they kept clear of the coast line. Evidence of early farming settlements were found at Aller Farm, Smallacombe, Lidewell and Higher and Lower Southwood.

The name of Dawlish has developed over the years, the earliest spelling recorded is 'Doflisc' (Anglo-Saxon) or 'Dolfishe' (Latin), The exact meaning or derivation is unknown although it is thought to have meant 'a fruitful mead in a bottom, or on a river's side'. Throughout the 1st century Dawlish was referred to by many names, but before that Dawlish had been synonymous with 'Devil Water' and after with 'Meadowland by Running Water', the latter being the motto adopted in the 20th century by the local council. Other local history will tell that the name 'Devil Waters', manifested from the red waters which flow from the hills after heavy rain - this still happens today and it is quite frequent to find the stream running through the town bright red in colour after heavy winter rains.

At the time Deawlisc (Dawlish) was a poor community, there was virtually no way of travel, the only ways in or out would have been over very rough cart tracks on to Haldon. Early maps show one track headed towards Luscombe Hill and on towards the Teignmouth direction and one went in the direction of Ashcombe and towards Exeter. A more substantial track existed between the port towns of Exeter and Teignmouth and was met by the tracks out of the Dawlish community.

When Leofric died in 1072 he gave his Manor of Dawlish lands to the Dean and Chapter of Exeter Cathedral. The area then remained under Church control until 1807. After Leofric's Death in 1072, Dawlish is mentioned in the Doomsday book, outlining the land and property owned by Bishop Osbern, Leofric's successor. It quotes that the bishop had 30 villeins (a villein was a person bound to the land and owned by the feudal lord), eight bordars, three serfs, three cows, two swine, 100 sheep, a coppice three furlongs in length and one in breadth, six acres of meadowland and 12 acres of pasture. It was valued at just £8 a year.

The Doomsday entry shows that Dawlish had cultivated land with sheep as its main wealth. The villeins would have lived in cob houses that clustered around the church and worked the Bishop's land. They would have lived mainly off beans, fruit and hard bread with lard whenever they could get hold of it. Local cider and beer would have been produced, providing a safer source of liquid than the water at the time.

The population of around 400 in 1080 grew only slowly, sickness was rife and the only real developments came as land was improved and better food became available. Records show that the Black Death, or Bubonic Plague, came to Dawlish in the 1340s and 1350s which almost wrote off the entire local population. By this time some more wealthy gentry were starting to emerge, and these people were able to escape the effects of the plague as they seldom left their estates, not coming into contact with the sick working classes. The plague returned to Dawlish again in 1629.

The Industrial Revolution, when it arrived in Dawlish, made significant changes to life, and the village quickly developed into a small town. The first industrial change was the operation of two flour mills, powered by water wheels, fed from the water course through the town. One, built in the late 1600s was located in what is now Brunswick Place and the other, in around 1730 in Church Street. A further mill was located near to Ashcombe.

By the end of the 18th century life in coastal towns such as Dawlish was starting to change for ever, the fear of the sea was receding and people started to extoll the virtues of fresh sea air and possible healing qualities from the sea waters. Dawlish found itself fashionable with the well off or gentry. At the time travel was virtually impossible and the gentry were

Below: *A very early picture of Dawlish station, dated 1861, shows the overall roof covered platform line with a west bound train, while the Sea Wall 'loop' track nearest the sea has been built and the iron supports we see today can be seen. The Atmospheric engine house is located in the goods yard and a number of bathing huts are seen on the beach.* **Author's Collection**

the only group who could afford to travel via private coach. Few indications exist, but it is widely considered that Dawlish did not have a regular (if you could call it that) stagecoach until around 1812.

The new wealthy visitors to Dawlish changed the face of life for the area for ever, with transport so difficult visitors arrived for long durations often with extended families complete with servants typically for an entire summer season. In terms of town development this was fruitful, for many enjoyed the area, purchased land and built new property. The types of Cobb-built cottage properties in the village at the time were not what the gentry sought and thus the area of residence spread further, especially along the banks of the Brook. Soon a number of fine houses and even villas were built using new and improved methods of construction allowing the previously unthought of position for many adjacent to the sea. Indeed some early documentation actually refers to 'sea views' and bathing potential!

After sea bathing was recognised as a healthy and pleasurable past time, it was still very much a gentleman's 'hobby'. Ladies seem not to have been welcome to sea bathe until the latter part of the 19th century.

By 1803 Dawlish development was moving forward fast, Dawlishownian John Manning masterminded improving the land either side of the stream or Brook which ran right down the middle of the community, which eventually allowed modern houses to be built closer to the sea front. His work physically straightened the town's water course, while embankments were built. This work led to the development of a new street, Pleasant Row, which is now known as The Strand.

Many people often wonder why the two main

Above: *An early etching of a line blockage near Parsons Tunnel around 1851, showing a rock fall from the unstable sandstone cliff face with a 4-4-0 loco being held while the line was cleared.* **Author's Collection**

roads of Dawlish, either side of the town, are so far apart, even with the relatively narrow water course down the middle. The reason lies in the problem of flooding, which although slightly controlled, has never gone away, even today. Heavy rain on the hills to the back of the town builds up both capacity and speed as they rush downhill towards the open sea. If a high tide, compounded by a south west wind hits at the same time the water from the hills has no where to go and floods the lower part of the town.

One of the first reported incidents of serious flooding causing major damage was in 1810 when fast flowing waters washed away eight new bridges, much of the then newly created public lawns, embankments and two residential properties in what is now Brook Street. After this disaster The Brook was altered, and weirs built to prevent a recurrence. At this time, the

Below: *The present view of Dawlish station from the west, showing an Arriva Cross Country Class 221 'Voyager' set passing the station on 12 July 2008 forming a Newcastle to Plymouth service.* **Author**

Left: *The view showing the original tunnel on the eastern approaches to Teignmouth. This was opened out and the present Skew bridge built in 1884.* **Author's Collection**

Below: *A Great Western poster as displayed at Paddington station well into BR days advertising the Royal Hotel in Teignmouth and the Rougemont Hotel in Exeter.* **Author's Collection**

which became less gentrified and more suited to the lower classes. The one and two week annual paid holiday became the norm and more and more people wanted to travel to the seaside town, mainly by train. At around the same time wealthy folk from industrial areas, especially London, Birmingham and Liverpool started to visit or retire to the area, this all leading to the once elegant villas being turned into hotels and guest houses.

The area just east of Dawlish, which became known as Dawlish Warren owes its success to the Great Western Railway who first built a station known as Warren Halt close to Langstone Rock in 1905. Prior to this, only a few large houses and mansions were to be found on the hill behind the Warren. By 1929, with the introduction of air travel, Dawlish even had an airport! The Great Western Railway built a small aerodrome on Haldon, to serve the greater Torbay area on a Cardiff to Plymouth route. The Second World War saw an end to the poorly patronised service. However, the

grass area in the middle of the town was still grazed by sheep.

As Queen Victoria arrived on the throne, early plans were being drawn up to bring the railway to the town. A number of propositions were put forward in the 1830s, which led to the building and opening of Isambard Kingdom Brunel's Atmospheric Railway in 1846. The railway suddenly brought new life to the town. Many hundred 'navvies' worked on construction of the line by digging cuttings and boring tunnels.

One of the most momentous days in Dawlish history was on Saturday 30 May 1846 when the first passenger train operated; by todays standards it was slow, but the news paper of the period hailed the train "taking only 40 minutes to reach Dawlish from Exeter". It is fascinating that the opening of the railway made Dawlish the first seaside resort to be served by railway west of Weston-super-Mare.

At the time, long distance transport was very much the preserve of the upper classes. The majority of people toiled six days a week and had to attend church once or twice on Sundays. Little time existed for people to visit the seaside except at Bank Holidays.

Development of Dawlish slowed towards the end of the 19th century, but increased wealth for the town meant that living standards improved and saw the introduction of gas, a

usable water supply, sewerage systems, and even street lighting. Household electricity was also laid on for those with sufficient funds.

Protection and safety of town folk also improved with a police office opening in 1857, (which is more than the town has today). A Coastguard look-out was opened in 1868 to provide some protection for mariners.

In 1906 a New Zealander introduced the now famous black swans to Dawlish Water or The Brook. John Nash, a Dawlish-born man who emigrated during adulthood but paid frequent visits to the town decided that the town needed some form of uniqueness. The Black Swans are still to be found on Dawlish Water, but today are supplemented by dozens of other species.

In the early 1900s, some workers from bigger businesses and employees of the gentry began to receive paid holidays. This saw a major upturn in visitor numbers to the town, with some deciding after a couple of visits to settle in the area. These increases in numbers saw some smaller housing erected (quite large by todays standards) in streets such as Luscombe Terrace and Hatcher Street, while open spaces in other 'older' roads was built over with quality housing. World War I stopped most further building until the early 1920s.

After the First World War was over, Dawlish became even more established for the day tripper. This had an adverse effect on town life

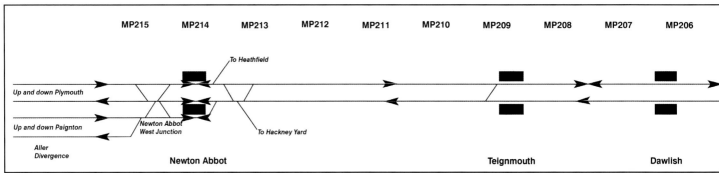

airport remained in use for many years under military control. Remnants of the old airfield can still be seen today.

By the 1930s Dawlish had become popular as a low budget holiday resort with holiday camps and caravans turning up. The railway played a major role in this, bringing literally thousands and thousands of people to the area every summer, with through trains from most corners of the UK.

The outbreak of World hostilities again in 1939 brought further development to a halt and considerably slowed down holiday travel. The Second World War also ended a plan which could have seen the railway disappear as we know it from Dawlish sea front, with plans put forward by the Great Western Railway to build a Dawlish 'cut-off' from Powderham via Gatehouse and Weech Road, making Dawlish served by a branch line. If this plan had been furthered, it would have gone right through the author's house!

In 1953, the year Queen Elizabeth II took the throne, the town of Dawlish adopted the Latin phrase 'Pratum Juxta Rivos Aquarum' as its motto, which translates (literally) as 'Meadowland by Running Waters'. The heraldic emblem of the town incorporates the arms of Edward the Confessor (top left: a cross patonce between five martlets, blue in colour), those of Leofric (top right: a dark cross with a bishop's mitre at the centre), and of the See of Exeter (bottom: an erect sword in pale argent surmounted by two keys) [See illustration on page 39}.

Holiday travel started to resume after World hostilities ended in 1945, with massive growth in holiday trade in the 1950s. This generated much business for the newly formed British Railways and remained through the early 1960s. By the 1970s, the town and surrounding area was starting a major change; the annual UK holiday was becoming a thing of the past, with low-cost, easily-accessible air travel tempting the previous UK holiday maker to seek pastures new. The hotels started to close and be demolished, to be replaced by retirement and second home accommodation, to such an extend that by 2008 Dawlish only has just one hotel of merit!

The guesthouse market was also adversely affected by the changing holiday patterns with

properties sold off for cheap one-room housing, while others have been demolished and rebuilt as high-price nursing homes. The vast majority of remaining holiday accommodation in the area now concentrates on huge camp sites offering a range of packages from self-catering holidays to sites to pitch your own van or tent. It is said that the camp sites in and around Dawlish, Dawlish Warren, Starcross and Teignmouth offer a staggering 18,000 beds. ■

Above: *The original station at Teignmouth showing the overall roof, viewed from the east end.* **Author's Collection**

Below: *Dawlish has only ever had one serious rail crash, that was on 22 September 1921 when a Plymouth to Crewe passenger train powered by GW 'Star' class No. 4055* Princess Sophia *emerged from Kennaway Tunnel and collided with goods wagons awaiting entrance to the station yard. The passenger train had overrun a signal at danger.* **Author's Collection**

Below: *A simplified track diagram of the Newton Abbot to Exeter route, the black arrows showing the signalled direction of travel. Map as at 2008. Not to scale.*

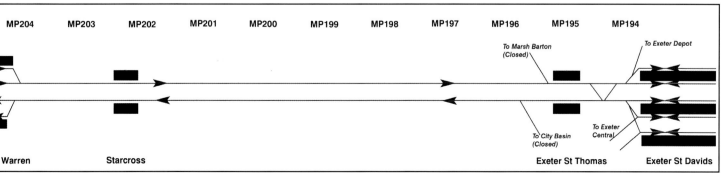

COWLEY BRIDGE (EXETER) TO STARCROSS

From Cowley Bridge Junction, where the former L&SWR (Southern) route to the west diverged from the ex-GW main line through to Exeter St Davids station is today a two track (one 'up' and 'one' down) railway. The line was first opened in 1844 as part of the Bristol & Exeter Railway. The L&SWR route arriving a few years later in 1851. Access to and from the Crediton line at Cowley Bridge is now via a ladder crossing arrangement.

Just west of Cowley Bridge Junction, access to Exeter Riverside Yard is located, this is today seldom used apart from the off-loading of occasional ballast trains from the Mendips, running round of ballast trains travelling to or from Meldon Quarry and recessing EWS freight services *en route* from the South West to South Wales and the Midlands.

For several years until 2008 Exeter Riverside yard was used as a storage ground for out of use freight and van stock, but this use has now ceased.

Exeter Riverside yard looks a mess today with the entire site weed infested and many of the original buildings now in decay.

On the opposite side of the running lines, nearer to Exeter St Davids station in Exeter West Yard, where South West Trains stable between duties on the Waterloo route, the sidings are occasionally used by First Great Western local services and Network Rail/Serco track inspection trains.

Directly at the London end of Exeter St Davids station is Red Cow level crossing; this is a very busy road linking the city and station side of Exeter with the Exwick residential area. The single barrier full width gates are controlled by Exeter Power Signal Box, but a crossing keeper is retained to locally control pedestrian traffic. A fascinating line indicator is located adjacent to the crossing which, when a signal is cleared for a move over the crossing, sounds a bell and the track number and direction is displayed.

Huge rationalisation of the Exeter St Davids area took place in the mid 1980s as part of the West of England resignalling project, which culminated in the two lines furthest away from the main station building becoming the 'up' and 'down' main lines, while those closer to the station amenities became the Waterloo bound lines and used for local services.

Above: *Pulling off the Crediton line at Cowley Bridge Junction, with the Great Western route to Tiverton disappearing off to the right, BR Standard Class 4 Tank No. 80080 pulls onto the 'up' main line before crossing over to the 'down' track with a Barnstaple to Exeter steam charter on 1 May 1994. The train is seen crossing over the River Exe, which after heavy and prolonged rain has been the cause of serious flooding in recent years, washing away the line a number of times.* **Author**

Left: *A road bridge carrying the A377 over Cowley Bridge Junction offers an excellent photographic viewpoint which, before lineside vegetation grew, allowed the picturesque Cowley Bridge Inn to be included in pictures. First GBRf Class 66/7 No. 66716* Willesden Traincare Centre, *rounds Cowley Bridge on 13 April 2005 powering off-lease ex-Network SouthEast liveried 4CIG No. 1399 as the 10.45 Clapham Junction Yard to Meldon Quarry. The unit was destined for store, having just been taken out of traffic on the Waterloo routes.* **Author**

Above: *With the Great Western 44-lever Cowley Bridge Junction signalbox in the foreground, which was closed on 30 March 1985, large-logo Class 50 No. 50022* Anson *rounds the curve under restricting signals on 6 July 1984 forming the 13.40 London Paddington to Penzance service.* **Author**

Right: *The once busy Exeter Riverside yard, located between Exeter St Davids and Cowley Bridge was once a hive of activity with general merchandise and block load trains and sported loading and unloading facilities for virtually any cargo. Today, the yard is weed infested and looks more like a grass playground, only being used for running round aggregate trains to/from Meldon Quarry, unloading occasional ballast trains and en route stabling of through freight services. A more recent visitor to the yard has been Freightliner, which is responsible for some Network Rail stone train operations in the area in conjunction with the High Output Ballast Cleaner (HOBC), out-based at Taunton Fairwater. No. 66581 is seen in Exeter Riverside Yard on 11 May 2006.* **Kevin Wills**

Adjacent to Exeter St Davids station is Exeter motive power depot, over the years this has seen many uses from providing power to operate local services in the 1950s-70s, stabling local multiple unit stock, servicing locos used on the Waterloo to Exeter route, servicing shunting power used in the local area to today, when the modernised facility is the principal First Great Western DMU depot in the West Country, officially housing the entire allocation of 14x and 15x DMMUs used through Devon and Cornwall. In 2008 extensive modernisation of the facility was ongoing, with a mechanised washing plant and improved servicing facilities installed.

Also adjacent to Exeter St Davids station is Exeter Power Signal Box, built in the 1980s as part of the West of England resignalling project. This box controls the lines from a point between Bridgwater and Cogload Junction on the Bristol route, Athelney on the line towards Castle Cary, Crediton on the Barnstaple/Meldon route, Exeter St James Park on the route to Exmouth/Honiton, Paignton, and to a point just west of Totnes on the main line.

West from Exeter St Davids the line travels out of the City on an elevation serving the suburb of St Thomas with today a two track bus-stop type station, which is just a shadow of its former glory when it once sported an overall roof. Directly west of Exeter St Thomas the remnants of the junctions for Exeter City Basin and Marsh Barton spur which once formed the connection with the Teign Valley line to Chudleigh and Newton Abbot closing in 1958 can be found.

Onward from Exeter St Thomas the twin route winds through the Exeter residential and industrial areas via Alphington towards Exminster, today passing under the M5 just before the former Exminster station, closed in 1964 is reached.

Exminster sported both 'up' and 'down' loops until the West of England resignalling, these were very useful for the recessing of freight traffic, but as this has now declined to just a handful of trains, such luxuries are no longer offered.

After Exminster the line shirts between the River Exe and the Powderham Estate, past the site of the steam era Exminster water troughs. After passing Powderham Castle, which can be clearly seen from passing trains, the line rounds towards Starcross. A one 'up' one 'down' platform station serving the local community as well as a ferry connection to Exmouth. Today, the station buildings are largely gone, with just 'bus-stop' facilities for passengers. Part of the station building has been taken over for retail use. A footbridge crossing the line here which offers excellent views of the line, the original Atmospheric railway engine house building and the Exe estuary.

The section of line between Exeter and Teignmouth first opened on 30 May 1846 and extended to Newton Abbot from December of the same year using Broad Gauge (7ft) track. It was operated using atmospheric pressure for propulsion between 23 February and 20 September 1848, from when it reverted to steam propulsion. It was converted to standard gauge from 1892. ∎

Right Top: *For many years the westbound 'main' platform at Exeter St Davids was the platform face adjacent to the main entrance. However as part of rationalisation in the 1980s involving the West of England re-signalling, this changed, and the traditional main line was moved to the island platform of the station. Taken on 5 June 1949, GW 51xx 2-6-2T No. 5132 departs west with an all stations service for Paignton. Note the second vehicle of the train is a Great Western 'Dreadnought'.* **J. P. Wilson**

Right Below: *There have been few more popular classes of diesel loco to grace the UK rail network than the Swindon/Crewe-built Type 4 'Western' diesel-hydraulic, later BR Class 52 fleet. Storming out of the 'down' main platform on 9 July 1970, No. D1018* Western Buccaneer *leads a Paddington to Plymouth express, while a Plymouth area DMMU No. 408 waits at the island platform with a stopping service.* **Norman E. Preedy**

Below: *For many years the 'up' Waterloo bound services from Exeter St Davids via Yeovil and Salisbury, in the hands of 'Warship' diesel-hydraulic locos, departed from the island platform, frequently loaded to eight or nine Mk1s. Today the same service is operated by three or six-car Class 159s. On 22 May 1971 maroon-liveried No. D817* Foxhound *awaits departure and the climb to Exeter Central with the 10.15 service to London Waterloo.* **Norman E. Preedy**

Above: With the long closed National Carriers Limited depot sign illuminated in the background, 'Western' Class 52 No. D1023 Western Fusilier awaits a misty departure from Exeter St Davids on 12 February 1977 with train 1Z54 the 06.30 Exeter St Davids to York. On the outward run the loco hit a herd of cows on the line near Charfield and had to be repaired by placing a 10p coin in the brake pipe to block a leak. **Author**

Left Middle: On summer Saturdays in the mid-1970s a through train from London Paddington to Barnstaple operated, which from Exeter St Davids was usually powered by a Class 31. However, on 11 September 1976, as no Type 2 was available and 'Western' No. D1065 was 'on shed' at Exeter, this was used on the Exeter to Barnstaple section. The loco is seen reversing onto the train while a 'Peak' is seen in the dead end siding outside Exeter Middle Box. **Author**

Left Bottom: The North British Type 2 diesel-hydraulics, later BR Class 22s, were never strong in Exeter area, but could be found from time to time on both passenger and freight services. On 9 April 1969, BR rail blue-liveried No. D6354 departs from the 'down' main platform at Exeter St Davids with an all stations service to Paignton, formed of no fewer than nine coaches including a buffet car. **D. J. H. Aston**

Above: *The depot adjacent to Exeter St Davids station, which over the years has had a variety of shed codes ranging from EXR under Great Western coding, 83C by BTC/BR from 1948 to 1973 when it was deemed as a stabling point. However, in more recent years following privatisation the depot has resumed a major maintenance role and now has an allocation of DMU stock for FGW local services, with the shed code EX used. After railtour duties on 24 May 1992, Class 50s Nos. D400 (50050), 50007 and 50033 stand in the siding between Exeter St Davids and Exeter depot, while a Class 108 DMMU is stabled behind.* **Author**

Right Upper: *In the days of Class 33s and 50s operating on the Waterloo to Exeter via Salisbury route the locos received fuel and a service check within the confines of Exeter depot. On 16 April 1991, NSE-liveried No. 50027* Lion *and two-car DMMU set No. P957 share depot space.* **Author**

Right Middle: *In 2008 Exeter depot was undergoing some major upgrade work to provide a coach washing facility and improved maintenance equipment to deal with DMU stock. Following the transfer of 12 ex-North Western Class 142 'Pacer' units to the depot in December 2007, which were knicknamed 'Donkeys' due to their tendency to bounce up and down when travelling at speed, the depot took on the name locally of the 'Donkey Sanctuary'.* **Author**

Right Bottom: *Exeter depot occasionally supplies fuel to other operators, such as Serco, DRS, EWS and Freightliner, the latter on a frequent basis when Class 66s operate into the area on empty aggregate trains and require fuel before returning on long distance heavy services. One such refuelling was on Sunday 22 June 2008 when No. 66625 worked light from Hackney Yard (Newton Abbot) to Exeter to collect fuel before working stone hoppers to Burngullow. In cases such as this the Freightliner driver 'buys' the fuel on a charge card - gone are the days on depots just 'topping up' locos as they arrive.* **Kevin Wills**

Left: *In the days of mechanical signalling at Exeter, Exeter Middle Box, located adjacent to Red Cow Crossing, dominated the landscape, with its little crossing keepers hut adjacent. Over the years three signalboxes have been named Exeter Middle, the final one opening in July 1914 and closing upon West of England re-signalling on 30 March 1985. This structure had an operating floor of 54ft x 12ft x 11ft 6in and had a total of 95 levers, not all of course were operational. This view shows the structure from the London end of the 'down' main platform on 28 August 1978.* **Graham Scott-Lowe**

Bottom: *Taken during the Exeter signalling transition period with colour lights erected but trains still controlled by semaphores, No. 50029 Renown approaches the 'up' main platform at Exeter St Davids on 12 June 1984 powering the 07.30 Penzance to Glasgow Central. Signs are displayed in the background for the construction work.* **Author**

Right: *The rather uninspiring Exeter Panel Signal Box (EX) is located at the west end of Exeter St Davids station and is a typical 1980s relay controlled box, obsolete before it even opened as by then solid state interlocking was the norm. The operating floor is on the upper level and the signalling staff have a good view of operations from the glazed windows directly above the box name. The relay room is located below.* **Inset:** *The main operating floor of Exeter Panel Box, controlling some 68 route miles of railway, with signallers, control staff and announcers having a clear observation of all movements. Both:* **Author**

Exeter home of the Met Office
St Davids

Above Film Strip: *Over the years a number of significant events have taken place at Exeter St Davids, these are just a small selection,* **1**. *Bernard Hughes, Vice Chairman of Devon County Council unveils the name* Devon Voyager *on the side of set No. 220030 on 22 February 2002.* **2**. *A new customer lounge was opened at the country end of platforms 5/6 in February 2007.* **3**. *Celebrity chief Brian Turner visited the station on 18 April 2007 to launch new FGW menus which involved cooking on platform 5/6.* **4**. *A poignant ceremony was held at Exeter St Davids on 25 June 2005 when powercar No. 43139 was named* Driver Stan Martin 25 June 1950 - 6 November 2004 *by his widow Deborah. Stan was killed in the Ufton Nervet accident in 2004. All:* **Author**

Right: *When the Class 142s operated in the West of England in the mid-1980s, all did not go well on the morning of 18 April 1987. Set No. 142017 was being shunted between roads at Exeter depot when it collided with the shunting neck buffer stops and partly went down the embankment towards the river. The Plymouth Laira tool vans attended and the set was rerailed by mid-day. This was the scene mid-morning with the staff and tool vans blocking the 'up' main line.* **Author**

Below: *The Great Western built station at Exeter St Davids is a sizeable structure, located on the downside of the line. The two storey building houses ticket, information, retail and staff accommodation on the ground floor including a British Transport Police office. Staff accommodation is also provided on the first floor. Still sporting its GWR logo near roof height, the station has been refurbished in recent years and is now finished in First Group colours.* **Author**

Left: *The first station opened at Exeter St Thomas on 30 May 1846 when the South Devon Railway opened its own facility, the station at Exeter St Davids being shared with the Bristol & Exeter Railway. Originally a single line station with a platform on the city side, it was enlarged in 1847 when the overall train shed was erected. The second 'up' platform was not built until 1861. A novel feature of this station originally was that only 'down' direction tickets were sold from St Thomas. 'Up' passengers could not board trains at this point and had to make their own way to St Davids station. This view taken in 1921 from the country end of the 'down' platform shows the magnificent roof structure. The buildings on the far right remain today but not for railway use.* **Author's Collection**

Above: *The overall train shed roof at Exeter St Thomas was demolished in the 1960s and today little more than 'bus stop' facilities exist. This is the view from the London end of the 'up' platform, showing Class 47/4 No. 47510 on 11 September 1982 leading the 11.05 Paignton to Paddington service. The 1861 built down side office and station building are still visible, while much of the down platform is original. Today, the station is served by most FGW local services on the Exeter to Paignton corridor and some South West Trains services.* **Author**

Below: *A very rare view of a down Broad Gauge passenger train running from Paddington to Plymouth is seen rounding the curve towards Exminster around 1890. Today, this is the point at which the M5 Motorway crosses the GW route, as shown in the colour inset view of a Class 158 and 150 passing in June 2003.* **Author/JAMV Collection**

Right Top: *Much recent building around the area of Exminster which has seen the outer boundaries of the City of Exeter extend westwards and has prompted many requests for the station to be reopened to serve the community. However, the site of the original station is a little out of the way and the only obvious point, near Gissons bridge, from where this view was taken, is liable to flooding. On 21 June 2006, a five-car Class 221 Virgin Super Voyager No. 221138 heads past the M5 bridge forming the 06.16 Preston to Plymouth service.* **Author**

Right Middle: *Exminster station was built by George Hennet and opened in August 1852, it was operated by him until 1857 when it was taken over by the South Devon Railway. The station was to Italian design and gradually enlarged until by 1931 it had four platform faces, with two fast lines and two loops. The station was closed by BR on 30 March 1964. While the station buildings saw further use, the platforms were removed. The signalbox, latterly an 80-lever frame remained in use until 15 November 1986. After closure the structure was used as a bird look out hide and not removed until 2007. EWS Class 67 No. 67015 passes the site of the former Exminster station and closed signal box on 15 July 2006 forming a returning charter, the 16.55 Par to Manchester Victoria formed of Pullman stock.* **Author**

Below: *Taken from the Exminster station roadbridge, which also served as the between-platform connection, this view looks towards Exeter and shows the layout in the early-1980s just before colour light signalling was commissioned. The down loop track was still in position, and outside the railway the Exminster by-pass 'Sannaville Way' was still under construction. The Gissons and M5 bridges are seen in the background. The train, powered by Class 47/0 No. 47018, is an additional advertised day charter 'ADEX' from Oxford to Paignton on 7 September 1983, formed of nine Mk1 coaches. At this time, before mass use of motor cars for long day trips had taken off, it was an almost a daily occurrence to find charter trains from various points within the Western Region to Paignton.* **Author**

Above: *The route west from Exminster follows the River Exe past the area known as Double Locks and the riverside public house of the same name, before reaching Powderham Crossing, where a public footpath crosses the line. Taken from the riverside defence wall by the public foot crossing, Regional Railways-liveried, Wales & West branded Class 150/2 No. 150253 forms the 09.10 Exeter St Davids to Paignton all stations service on 15 February 2003.* **Author**

Below: *The area around Powderham Castle and Estate, owned by the Courtenay family since 1391 and the present home of 18th Earl and Countess of Devon, is a charming picturesque corner of the County on the banks of the River Exe, with the rail line passing through a huge deer park and grounds. Excellent photographic opportunities exist around the area to capture passing trains, but the erection of high Network Rail fences in recent years has made this increasingly difficult. ETH fitted Class 31/4 No. 31410 approaches Powderham Crossing on 17 July 1982 forming the 16.35 Exeter St Davids to Paignton local service.* **Author**

Above: *Taken in the summer of 1930, a down London Paddington to Plymouth Millbay Docks Ocean Liner Express, formed of a wonderful array of Pullman Car Co stock, approaches Starcross station. Power is provided by GW 'Castle' 4-6-0 No. 4075 Cardiff Castle.*
Robert Brookman/Rail Archive Stephenson

Right Middle: *Starcross station, built by the South Devon Railway, was opened on 30 May 1846, it had a single platform, as illustrated during the period of atmospheric operation in 1848. The second platform was added at the end of 1848, and the overall train shed lasted until 1906 when the station area was rebuilt. The station, still open today, handled goods traffic until 1965 and coal traffic until 1967.*
Author's Collection

Right Bottom: *Directly at the west end of Starcross station was an atmospheric pumping (engine) house, which after the year long experiment of atmospheric propulsion, fell into disrepair from 1848. The building was later used as a Methodist Chapel, a youth club, coal store and in the 1980s a museum to the atmospheric railway system. Sadly the museum closed and today the building is used as the headquarters of the Starcross Fishing & Cruising Club. On 5 June 1969 a 'Warship' diesel-hydraulic passes between the pumping house and signalbox with a westbound engineers train.* **Terry Nicholls**

Below: *Today, Starcross station is virtually a bus stop with no station facilities. A modern steel footbridge replaced the original GW design in 1999 and provides a walkway to Starcross Pier, from where regular summer ferry sailings are made across the River Exe to Exmouth.* **Author**

Above: *Apart from the replacement of the lower quadrant semaphore signal with a colour light, different fencing and lighting and the removal of the pole route on the left side, this view of a 'down' train approaching Starcross has changed little over the last 54 years. In 1955 GW 'Modified Hall' 4-6-0 No. 6994* Baggrave Hall, *built to lot No. 368 in 1948, slows for the Starcross stop with a 'down' train formed of four ex-GW coaches.* **T G Hepburn/Rail Archive Stephenson**

Right Top: *With the main A379 Teignmouth-Dawlish-Exeter road on the left, this is the present view of Starcross station from the platform footbridge looking towards Exeter and the Powderham Estate. On the right is the River Exe, with Lympstone and Topsham on the eastern bank. With only bus stop facilities remaining, Class 220 Cross Country 'Voyager' No. 220022 hurries past the station on 25 May 2008 forming the 10.24 Manchester Piccadilly to Paignton. This set is painted in the latest XC brown and silver livery.* **Author**

Right Bottom: *A down First Great Western HST formation approaches Starcross station while an Arriva Cross Country 'Voyager' passes in the 'up' direction. Starcross station is mainly served by FGW and SWT local services, but a handful of FGW HSTs do stop at the station to provide a through London connection. As the station has short platforms, the conductor has to use the set's selective door opening system to release only doors adjacent to the platform.* **Author**

Below: *With the background dominated by the original Brunel atmospheric pumping (engine) house building, now used by the Starcross Fishing & Cruising Club, Voyager No. 220008, then still operated by Virgin Trains, storms through the station on 8 June 2007 forming the 17.25 Plymouth to Preston service. On top of the atmospheric tower, the Starcross Fishing & Cruising Club have a user operated 'webcam' providing views of the Exe Estuary, local area and railway. Note that at this point the signal number corresponds with the milepost Down Main (DM) 202.* **Author**

Starcross

First Great Western · THE RIVIERA LINE

HST STOP 2 + 8 Car

Dawlish Sea Wall: The Railway between Exeter and Newton Abbot

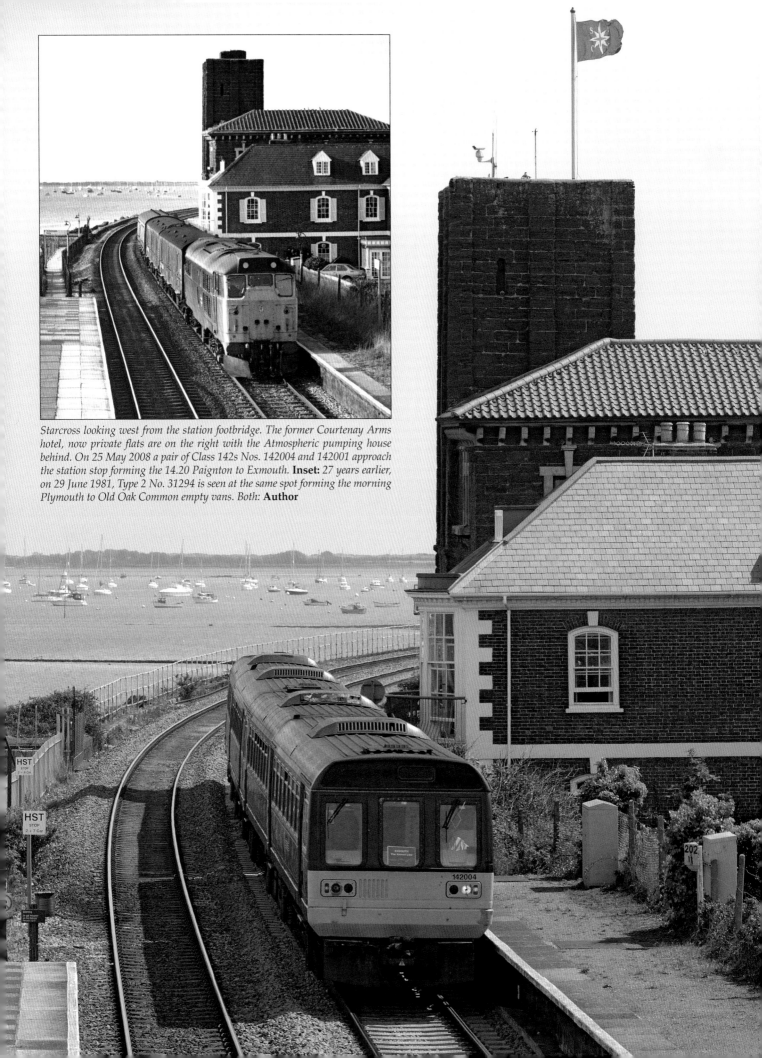

Starcross looking west from the station footbridge. The former Courtenay Arms hotel, now private flats are on the right with the Atmospheric pumping house behind. On 25 May 2008 a pair of Class 142s Nos. 142004 and 142001 approach the station stop forming the 14.20 Paignton to Exmouth. **Inset:** *27 years earlier, on 29 June 1981, Type 2 No. 31294 is seen at the same spot forming the morning Plymouth to Old Oak Common empty vans. Both:* **Author**

COCKWOOD HARBOUR AND EXE ESTUARY

Just to the west of Starcross lay the village of Cockwood and Cockwood Harbour, without any doubt the most photographed location on the Dawlish Sea Wall route between Exeter and Newton Abbot.

Cockwood is a small village sporting two pubs, The Ship Inn and The Anchor, both offer excellent food and drink, but few other amenities exist.

The railway crosses over the harbour on a causeway, which originally had three bridge openings to allow small craft into an inner harbour, however only two remain today. The open sea side of the causeway is actually the Exe Estuary which houses hundreds of river and sea craft and is a popular sailing area.

Since the railway route first opened through Cockwood in 1846, small embankments on both sides of the inner harbour have provided

excellent photographic vantage points for both 'up' and 'down' trains depending on the time of day. However in late 2007 Network Rail decided to erect a white fence along the top of the causeway effectively ruining all subsequent photographs.

The line in this area is formed of one up and one down line and follows the main A379 road from Starcross to Cockwood Harbour. The line, after crossing the water, then follows a back road to Dawlish Warren via Cofton and Eastdon, which also provides some good vantage points of the line. A public foot crossing is located adjacent to the small village of Cofton which provides access to the foreshore at low tide.

It is interesting when standing at Cockwood and looking east towards Exeter, trains traversing the Exeter to Exmouth branch line (once part of

the Southern Railway route to Exmouth) can be seen and frequently heard if the wind is in the right direction.

The area around Starcross, Cockwood and towards Dawlish Warren is a special location in terms of wildlife. The estuary is designated as a Special Protection Area and a site of Special Scientific Interest, as well as being an internationally important location for wintering waterfowl with frequent sightings of Avocets, Slavonian Grebes, Brent Geese and Black-tailed Godwits.

For anyone wishing to visit Cockwood, restricted parking is possible on both sides of the harbour, but good public transport is provided by Stagecoach Devon with their route 2 from Exeter to Newton Abbot passing along the main road. ∎

Right: *The residents and traders of Cockwood Harbour provide a fine floral display along the side of the harbour wall by the Anchor Inn during the summer months, from where many rail enthusiasts can sit and enjoy a quiet drink and watch passing trains. On 3 September 2007 a westbound Class 150/2 crosses the causeway bound for Paignton.* **Author**

Below: *Freight traffic these days is a shadow of its former quantity, but in recent years a slight increase has been recorded with extra Freightliner Heavy Haul-operated aggregate trains from Cornwall for use in construction of the Olympic Village in East London. On 6 September 2007, Class 66/6 No. 66620 crosses Cockwood Harbour powering additional train 6Z60, the 10.51 Neasden to Newton Abbot Hackney Yard.* **Author**

Above: *Usually photographers recording trains crossing Cockwood Harbour concentrate on just the train and immediate surrounding area. On 12 August 2007 when the returning 'Torbay Express' charter from Kingswear to Bristol approached the harbour at around 18.30 the sun dipped and the author decided to change lens and use a 17mm wide angle to record the entire vista of the harbour with the train on the far left side. The image was considerably helped by having water in the harbour and the pleasing blue and cloudy sky. This view shows almost the entire village of Cockwood, with the Anchor Inn in the harbourside with a number of drinkers outside enjoying the evening. The smokebox of ex-GW 'King' 4-6-0 No. 6024* King Edward I *is at the location of the original third bridge entrance to the inner harbour.* **Author**

Left Below: *In the days when Virgin Trains were still operating loco-hauled services to supplement HST workings on its Cross Country network, restored green-liveried Class 47 No. 47851* Traction Magazine *passes Cockwood on 14 September 2002 leading the Summer Saturday 11.11 Birmingham New Street to Paignton, a train formed of a hired-in West Coast set complete with Mk.3 DVT No. 82121 on the rear.* **Author**

Below: *Operating as a 'stand-in' for a First Great Western HST, Class 47 No. 47832 Tamar, a rake of Mk.2 stock and No. 47813 on the rear cross over a well filled Cockwood Harbour on 13 July 2003 forming the 15.41 Penzance to Paddington service. The positioning of boats and especially any with tall masts is all important in composing pictures at this location, to ensure nothing obscures any part of the train image. By the looks of the front window of this service some haulage enthusiasts were enjoying the non-HST ride.* **Author**

Left: *Crossing over the original middle entrance to the inner harbour at Cockwood, ex-GWR 68xx 'Grange' No. 6813* Eastbury Grange *built in 1936 heads the 17.30 stopping service from Kingswear to Exeter St Davids on 8 June 1949. The evening light at this location favours the 'up' view. In the steam era photographers did not use Cockwood that frequently as a telegraph pole line, seen on the right, obstructed some of the picture if the photographer stood too far back from the subject.* **E. D. Bruton**

Below: *Each year the superbly restored Venice Simplon Orient-Express (VSOE) UK-based Pullman train makes a weekend trip to the West Country, usually operating west from London to Cornwall and then working one or two local dining trains. On 7 July 2007, powered by Class 67 No. 67013 the train crosses Cockwood forming charter 1Z32, the 18.49 Exeter St Davids to Kingswear dinner special.* **Author**

Above Film Strip: *Dozens and dozens of different train types have been recorded at Cockwood over the years, the author has recorded over 120 variations. Just a small selection are shown here.* **1**. *The classic view of a 'down' refurbished MTU-powered HST crossing the harbour on 14 September 2007.* **2**. *In 2007 Cross Country hired-in Midland Mainline branded HSTs to power two Saturday West of England services which could not be covered by strengthened Voyager diagrams. Now under Arriva Cross Country control, a small fleet of HSTs are in service forming the most popular trains.* **3**. *Celebrity Class 47 No. 47840* North Star *was a frequent visitor to the Sea Wall in Spring/Summer 2007 powering FGW Mk3 refurbished stock moves; here the loco is seen with a pair of Mk.2 barrier cars.* **4**. *Heading for Exeter and Exmouth, an unrefurbished Wessex-liveried Class 150/2 crosses the harbour in July 2007.* All: **Author**

Above: *Until the erection of the unsightly and totally unnecessary fence over Cockwood Harbour in autumn 2007, the location was popular with photographers recording evening charters returning from the west, especially the summer steam specials when the tide was in. One of the finest preserved steam crossings observed by the author passing Cockwood was on 26 August 2007 when 'King' No. 6024* King Edward I *led the return Kingswear to Bristol 'Torbay Express', with a high tide and smoke. On that evening some 250 observers stood, watched and photographed the train in near perfect summer evening conditions.* **Author**

Below: *To many, the HST fleet looked their best when painted in InterCity 'Swallow' livery, with the number applied below the cab window. In the days when Velenta engines reigned supreme, No. 43088 heads west at Cockwood on 5 June 1993 forming the 10.05 Paddington to Paignton. This CrossCountry powercar, allocated to Laira was being used on Great Western services due to a stock shortage.* **Author**

DAWLISH WARREN AND LANGSTONE ROCK

The area on the Sea Wall known as Dawlish Warren did not have its own railway station until the summer of 1905 when a small halt, named Warren Halt, with platforms just 150ft long were opened, which were extended a year later to 400ft in length. Some two years after, small offices were provided and the station was renamed Warren Platform. These facilities were not located at the site of the present Dawlish Warren station, but adjacent to the present footbridge which crosses the line between the car park at Dawlish Warren and the sea wall leading to Langstone Rock.

It was not until 1 October 1911 that the station was officially renamed Dawlish Warren. It was soon found to be inadequate for patronage and a new station located on loop lines was opened on 23 September 1912. This facility had platforms 600ft long and was located a quarter of a mile the Exeter side of the original structure.

The new station sported buildings on both the 'up' and 'down' side, with vehicular access on the 'up' side. The station buildings on the down side were destroyed by fire on 9 January 1924. A signal box was also located on the westbound platform, which opened when the loop lines were built in 1911 and remained in use until the West of England resignalling in 1986. A footbridge was provided between up and down platforms, which was removed in the 1980s, meaning passengers had to use the underbridge between the sides of the station. Part of the footbridge deck was later reused near Torre on the Newton Abbot to Paignton line.

A small goods yard was located at the country end of the new Dawlish Warren station and within its confines a camp coach was positioned from the summer of 1935, but by 1940 the facility was withdrawn.

After a short period, public camping coaches returned between 1942-53 and by the summer of 1959 nine bogie carriages available. In 1964 the

British Railways (Western Region) camping coach service was withdrawn, with the carriages at Dawlish Warren taken over by the BR Staff Association. The original GW vehicles were worn out by 1982 and replaced by rebuilt Mk.1s and inspection saloons, which were prepared by Swindon Works and positioned in the old goods yard. Today these are operated privately.

The goods yard at Dawlish Warren remained operational with diminishing receipts until

Above: *With Dawlish Warren goods yard on the left, the location later taken by camping coaches, and a very spartan landscape at Dawlish Warren on the right, GW 'Castle' 4-6-0 No. 5092* Tresco Abbey, *built in April 1938, powers west on 2 June 1952 with the 'Torbay Express'. At this time the station buildings, footbridge and platelayers' hut were still in daily use. The area to the right of the train was extensively built in the 1960s and 70s to provide shops and holiday maker amenities, some wooden-built shops were removed in the 1990s due to fire risk, but today the sea front area even sports a public house.*
Michael E. Ware

Above Film Strip: 1. *The original footbridge over the line in the location of the original Warren Halt.* **2**. *The sole passenger amenity on the down platform in 2008 - a closed ticket office.* **3**. *The burnt out remains of the down platform after the 2003 fire.* **4**. *The new residential 'box' on the 'up' platform built in 2007-08. All:* **Author**

Above: *If this is compared with the view from the same location on the opposite page a number of significant changes will be seen - building on the right side, no footbridge, different signalling, altered track layout and camping coaches placed in the former yard. Taken on 6 May 2008 this view shows the 16.05 Paddington to Penzance led by refurbished power car No. 43093. The remains of a boarded engineers accommodation crossing can be seen under the first coach. Discussions have been held to resurrect this as a permanent feature to allow emergency vehicles access to the Dawlish Warren peninsula.* **Author**

closure in August 1967 and four years later the station became unstaffed.

With loop platforms for stopping trains, Dawlish Warren is frequently used to allow fast or main line services to overtake slow passenger or freight trains. The buildings on the 'up' side were, after closure, used to house the Dawlish Warren Railway Museum, but this closed in 1984 and the buildings were converted to holiday accommodation. Sadly the structure was destroyed by fire on the night of 15 June 2003. In 2007/08 a new structure of like design to Dawlish Warren GW signal box was built on the site of the original 'up' side buildings.

A walkway exists along the side of the railway the entire way from Dawlish Warren to Dawlish and beyond. The path is accessed from either the sea front or the original railway footbridge and leads along to Langstone Rock, also known as 'Red Rock'.

The area around Langstone Rock offers some outstanding views of trains in both directions rounding the tight curve at the foot of the rock. It is possible to climb to the top of Langstone Rock, but by 2008 the eroding steps were becoming something of a problem, however, several small hills at the base of the rock are still available.

No amenities had ever existed on the sea wall, but in the late 1990s a small cafe took over the lease of a building at the foot of Langstone Rock and opened this as the Red Rock Cafe. This now has a thriving trade in hot and cold food and drinks. It is very enthusiast friendly and is acknowledged by a high proportion of the trains that pass.

Access to the amenities at Dawlish Warren, including the golf club have always been a problem, as the rail overbridge at the country end of Dawlish Warren station has insufficient head room to allow anything through but a car or small van, therefore fire engines and the like do not have full access to the Warren area. Various considerations have been given to allowing special vehicles access over the tracks, but as this would require sophisticated interlocking with signalling, this would be a costly option. ∎

Below: *Throughout 2007 considerable extra non-revenue traffic traversed the Sea Wall route with empty stock and power car movements in conjunction with a major First Group fleet refurbishment programme. The Mk.3 stock was overhauled at either Bombardier Derby or Ilford Works, with power cars dealt with at the Brush Traction plant in Loughborough. In the main First/GBRf was contracted to power these stock moves. On 3 July 2007, First/GBRf Class 66/7 No. 66725 approaches Dawlish Warren station hauling seven refurbished HST trailer vehicles marshalled between two FGW Mk.2 barrier vehicles forming train 5Z90, the 13.00 Bombardier Derby to Laira depot.* **Author**

Left: *Passing the site of the original Warren Halt station, and pulling under the footbridge which is still in use today and refurbished by Network Rail in 2005-06, we see GW 28xx 2-8-0 No. 2855 powering an up potato train from Bodmin, Cornwall to the London markets. On the left is the 'down' main lower quadrant semaphore starting signal, complete with telegraph cables attached to the top of the finial. Loco No. 2855 was built at Swindon Works to lot No. 190 in 1913.* **E. D. Bruton**

Right: *With the buildings of the Dawlish Warren Golf Club on the far right, the station buildings adjacent to the train and the signalbox at the far end of the down platform, this was the view from the station footbridge at Dawlish Warren on 9 August 1955. The eight coach 10.36 Exeter St Davids to Kingswear all stations service stops to collect some passengers on a very wet summers day. The train is powered by BR Standard Class 4 4-6-0 No. 75028.* **P. Poulter**

Left: *Today, one of the better evening views of an 'up' train traversing the Sea Wall can be obtained from the original station footbridge at Dawlish Warren. With the use of a medium length telephoto lens some obstructive lineside furniture can be cropped from the foreground and the unmistakable outline of Langstone Rock included as a backdrop. The summer Sunday 'Torbay Express' trains always generate a lot of interest from locals and holiday makers, with youngsters frequently seeing their first 'real' steam loco powering a train at speed. On 23 July 2006, GW 'King' No. 6024* King Edward I *approaches the bridge at full line speed with a trailing load of 10 Mk.1 coaches.* **Author**

Right & Below: *In many cases the same views of the Dawlish Sea Wall which were recordable some 50-100 years ago are still available to us today, with in some cases little of the surrounding area having changed. One location which is immediately recognisable is Langstone Rock, just west of Dawlish Warren. Apart from the pole route going and some extra embankment vegetation little has changed in these two views. The upper picture, taken on 9 August 1956, shows the 05.30 Paddington to Penzance service, train No. 100, rounding the curve powered by GW 'Castle' No. 5023* Brecon Castle. *It is interesting to note that 50 years later the first London departure for the West was a whole two hours later! The view below shows the corresponding first train of the day from Paddington in 2008, when on 13 May 2008 the 07.30 Paddington to Penzance led by power car No. 43145 pounds west.*
Tom Williams/Author

Left Top: *The view is the same, but the trains are rather different. This was the style of local travel on the Sea Wall in the summer of 1957, with one of the then infrequent all stations stopping services between Exeter St Davids and Newton Abbot calling at Exeter St Thomas, Starcross, Dawlish Warren, Dawlish and Teignmouth. The train was formed of seven GW-design coaches and power was provided by GW 51xx class 2-6-2T No. 4174.*
A. R. Butcher

Left Middle: *Viewed from slightly higher up the hill side at Langstone Rock is this 9 August 1956 view of a westbound 12-coach extra service bound for Torbay. With a good head of steam, GW 51xx class 2-6-2T No. 4157 makes a fine sight. The footpath with the rock armour sea defences are much the same as today.* **R. J. Blenkinsop**

Below: *In 2008, viewed from the same location, this is what local West Country travel has turned into, nothing more than a bus on rail wheels! From December 2007, allegedly for a limited period only, a fleet of 12 ex-North Western Class 142 'Pacer' sets entered traffic on Devon branch lines, working the Exeter to Barnstaple, Exmouth, Paignton with some Plymouth services. Mainly working in pairs, the sets replaced Class 150 and 153 units which were the subject of refurbishment. The Class 142s with 2+3 bus style seating and a great tendency to squeal on all but straight and level track were not at first welcomed by passengers or staff; however, by mid-2008 their performance had improved and on several occasions a 100 per cent availability figure was returned. On 13 May 2008, set No. 142062 forms the 09.20 Exmouth to Paignton all stations service. At the time this illustration was taken, no roller-blind destination indicators were fitted and drivers/conductors used flip-over paper sheets to display the line of route propped up in the front middle window.* **Author**

Above & Below: *Two eras of Cross Country rail travel. Above we see the latest Arriva Cross Country brown and silver livery, off-set by pink doors and branding applied to the Class 220 and 221 'Voyager' fleet. Virgin first introduced these four and five car sets to replace between eight and 10-car formations in the early years of the century and faced huge criticism on the grounds of over-crowding and lack of luggage space. Set No. 220017 approaches Langstone Rock with Dawlish in the background on 12 May 2008 forming the 10.02 Paignton to Newcastle service. In the picture below at the same location, this was the view in June 1959 and shows Swindon-built 'Warship' Type 4 No. D806 Cambrian powering a Kingswear to Manchester through service. Over the years this view from the lower levels of Langstone Rock, looking towards Dawlish has changed little, except for considerable expansion of housing on the West Cliff side of the town.*
Author/Stan Creer

With the town of Dawlish in the background, EWS Class 67 No. 67022 approaches Langstone Rock on 21 August 2004 while forming the Virgin Trains, 08.43 Paignton to Preston Summer Saturday service. **Author**

Above: *With the Royal Navy Dockyard and DML Engineering based in Plymouth, a small amount of Nuclear traffic traverses the Sea Wall. Today, these trains are operated by Carlisle-based Direct Rail Services. In readiness to transfer a flask to Sellafield, Class 66/4s Nos. 66417 and 66415 pass Langstone Rock hauling escort carriages Nos. 9428 and 9419 on 13 May 2008 forming train 6Z73, the 04.22 Crewe Basford Hall to MoD Keyham.* **Author**

Left: *During the 1990s members of Class 56 and 60 became quite common powering freight services through Devon. Following the privatisation of the UK rail industry, fleet rationalisation, and the mass purchase of Class 66s, class variety in the west was lost with only very occasional visits by members of Class 60. On 10 September 1994, the day after the launch of the 'shadow' freight operations under BR, Class 56 No. 56044 and Class 60 No. 60097 both wearing Transrail markings, power an additional 10.35 St Blazey to Newport formed of exhibition wagons past Langstone Rock.* **Author**

Above Film Strip:
1. *Colas Class 47 No. 47727 passes Langstone in March 2008 running light from Worcester to Tavistock Junction.* 2. *Central Trains green-liveried Class 158 on hire to First Group.* 3. *A Teignbridge Council sign erected in 2008 at Langstone Rock identifying the adjacent beach as 'Red Rock Beach' a name which it has never had in the past.* 4. *Virgin Trains-liveried Class 47 (but operated by Freightliner) No. 47805 hauls power cars Nos. 43156, 43195, 43079 and 43063 past Langstone Rock, en route to St Philips Marsh on 13 September 2004.* All: **Author**

Right: *During World War II a number of War Department, or more correctly Ministry of Supply, 2-8-0s were built by the North British Loco Co and Vulcan Foundry and used on many routes in the UK. The Western Region was no exception and MoS 2-8-0s were seen from time to time traversing the Sea Wall. In this 1950 view No. 70801 is seen rounding the curve at Langstone Rock heading for Plymouth, with what was described by the photographer as a "fast freight".* **M. M. South**

Right Middle: *With the 1982 replacement camping coaches visible in the background, three-car Class 118 Birmingham RC&W built DMMU set No. P461 departs from the 'down' platform loop at Dawlish Warren on 1 July 1984 forming the 10.20 Exeter St Davids to Paignton service. The new gantry has already been erected for the colour light signalling.* **Author**

Below: *The wide Sea Wall walkway from Dawlish Warren extends all the way to Dawlish offering unrestricted views of the railway and providing some excellent photographic potential. In terms of photographic light the morning time is the best before the sun (if it is out) passes to the land side. Captured just at the point where the Langstone curve commences and turns the line towards the Exe Estuary, First Great Western's 07.43 Penzance to Paddington via Bristol service on 13 May 2008 led by power car No. 43170 with No. 43140 on the rear, passes under the bi-directional signal gantry. In the background is the Rockstone footbridge.* **Author**

THE DAWLISH SEA WALL AND DAWLISH

The Dawlish Sea Wall between Dawlish Warren and Dawlish emerged as part of the construction of the rail line west from Exeter by the South Devon Railway, in the mid-1840s to protect the line from the ravages of the sea. The line to Dawlish opened on 30 May 1846. Originally it was a single broad gauge track of (7ft 0¼ in) operated by atmospheric pressure until September 1848. From its opening the wall, which was built progressively from 1836, located between the rail track and beach was available for walkers between the two points and provided access to the increasingly popular bathing beaches.

In the main the wall is built at track height, except for a section opposite Sea Lawn Terrace, Dawlish, where it drops to virtually beach height, built in this way as the affluent residents and land owners of Sea Lawn Terrace did not want those 'peasants' walking the wall to be able to gawp into their property.

The single line railway between Dawlish Warren and Dawlish was doubled in May 1858 to meet traffic demands. Broad gauge track gave way to standard gauge lines from 22 May 1892.

The original Dawlish station, opened in 1846, on the same site as the present structure, was built of wood and iron, complete with an overall train shed which was burnt down on 14 August 1873. The present brick built structure was opened on 12 April 1875. Over the years many alterations have been made, the original steel glazed roof gave way to a concrete and perspex structure in 1961. The footbridge remains, providing the only link between the 'up' and 'down' side of the station. Today few passenger facilities exist; the booking office on the lower level is still open and daytimes the station platforms are manned.

Returning to the Sea Wall itself, roughly mid-way between Dawlish Warren and Dawlish a bridge linking the Exeter Road with the Sea Wall and Beach is provided. This was originally a concrete structure, replaced with a more modern wooden deck in the 1980s. Further towards Dawlish a metal single width footbridge existed until the early 1970s between Sea Lawn Terrace and the Sea Wall.

A Coastguards' lookout together with a boathouse below on the water line was erected in 1846 just to the London end of Dawlish station. This was originally manned by HM Preventative Services and later the Coastguard service. The Coastguard station closed in 1901 and the building together adjacent cottages became residential. In recent years the Coastguard building has been a restaurant and bar, while the boat house has been used for hiring out small water craft, but both were closed in 2008. A footbridge from the beach served the Coastguard building and provided further access to the main Exeter Road.

Dawlish station has by its position been the subject of many wash-outs over the years, with on numerous occasions parts of the down platform station fencing and even parts of the station buildings being washed away.

Dawlish boasted a busy goods yard, located on the 'up' side from station opening until 17 May 1965. The site is now the station car park, with office and workshop facilities for Network Rail and its contractors at the London end.

Directly west of Dawlish station the railway crosses the Colonnade Viaduct, which takes the line over a walkway to the Sea Wall and over Dawlish Water (The Brook), which divides the east and west sides of the town. The railway continues skirting Marine Parade to the first of five tunnels, Kennaway. The Sea Wall footpath continues on the sea side and from here to Kennaway Tunnel and Boat Cove is officially known as the King's Walk. Originally a wrought iron, now a steel and concrete footbridge crosses the portal of Kennaway Tunnel.

At this point the railway passes under Lea Mount, a tall land mass on which a number of footpaths exist, allowing walkers to climb the hill and gain excellent views of Lyme Bay and

Left: From an initial glance it looks as if a lot of people have turned out to see large logo Class 47 No. 47847 Brian Morrison head west in this view of the Sea Wall from the Rockstone Bridge on 29 March 2002. However, they were not actually interested in the train at all, the group was a walking party who were taking directions from the rather silly man standing on the wall, who a few seconds after this picture was taken was literally blown off the wall narrowly missing serious injury. In the background major sea defence work is seen under way, which included the building of extra levels of wall to reduce the impact of the sea against the main structure, the finished extra defences are seen in the foreground. **Author**

Below: *The Dawlish town Coat-of-Arms.* **Author**

PRATUM JUXTA RIVOS AQUARUM

Dawlish Town Council

the railway all the way from Dawlish Warren (Langstone Rock).

The other four tunnels travelling west are Coryton, Phillot, Clerks and Parsons, the latter emerging onto the Teignmouth Sea Wall.

Single line operation remained through the five tunnels west of Dawlish until 1902-05 when full double track operation was introduced, this delay was due to the amount of civil engineering work required to increase the tunnel openings, in several cases requiring the surrounding embankments to be shored up.

From the top of Lea Mount Gardens a good view of trains between the tunnels can be obtained, but sadly this is quickly becoming overgrown.

A popular view of trains emerging from Clerks Tunnel by Horse Cove which can be accessed from a footpath from Old Teignmouth Road. ■

Above: *With Langstone Rock in the background, this late 1950s view shows GW 28xx 2-8-0 No. 2861 heading west with a light freight. No. 2861 was built in 1918 at Swindon Works to lot No. 210. This view has not changed over the years and the same vista, albeit with a different train type, can be captured today.* **E. D. Bruton**

Below: *The Rockstone footbridge connecting the main Exeter Road with the Sea Wall has been a popular spot for photographers for well over 100 years. The scene has changed little, and the view is immediately recognisable. In the summer of 1932 GW 43xx class 2-6-0 No. 4353, built at Swindon in 1914, leads a four carriage local service towards Dawlish Warren and Exeter. The wall, cliff face and buildings in Sea Lawn Terrace and the Catholic Church above on the Exeter Road, are virtually the same today.*
H. Gordon Tidey/Rail Archive Stephenson

Above: *The end of loco-hauled passenger services on the Dawlish Sea Wall (apart from the overnight sleeper and charter services) came on 16 August 2002 when Virgin Trains operated their final loco-hauled Cross Country service. The train, the 08.46 Penzance to Manchester Piccadilly, was powered by celebrity Class 47 No. 47840* North Star *and is seen approaching The Rockstone Bridge. The train carried a special "Cross Country Locomotive Farewell" headboard.* **Author**

Left Middle: *The Class 45 and 46 'Peak' 1Co-Co1 fleet was very common in the West Country from the late 1960s powering both passenger and freight services. The locos' main operations involved the increasing number of through workings from the South West to the North East and North West, long before the Cross Country name came into vogue. On 13 June 1974, Class 45 'Peak' No. D31, later renumbered as 45030, approaches Rockstone Bridge powering a Paignton to Liverpool Lime Street working. The 'Peak' would have operated this service to Birmingham New Street from where an ac electric would take over for the remainder of the journey.* **Author**

Left Bottom: *During the 1980s the most popular loco class to traverse the Sea Wall was the English Electric Class 50, drafted in to replace the 'Western' Class 52s from the mid-70s. The fleet went on to power main line services to London, Cross Country services to Birmingham and operate the Plymouth/ Exeter to Salisbury and Waterloo route. Painted in 'large logo' livery, No. 50036* Victorious *approaches Rockstone Bridge on 20 April 1988 powering the 08.17 Paignton to Exeter St Davids. After arrival in Exeter the loco ran round its train and formed the 09.40 Exeter St Davids to Waterloo via Salisbury.* **Author**

Above: *Viewed coming from under the 1980s replacement Rockstone Bridge, now with wood decking and by 2008 looking somewhat the worse for more than 20 years exposure to all the elements, is a Class 142 'Pacer', with First Great Western branding applied to just one coach, but sporting roller-blind destination indicator, set No. 142067 forms the 09.14 Paignton to Exmouth via Exeter on 12 June 2008. The name Rockstone came from a public house and hotel built at the top of the footbridge steps and path on the Exeter Road, which was demolished in the 1970s and now high-quality private flats stand on the site, also known as Rockstone. This bridge is also known to locals as 'Black Bridge'* **Author**

THE SEAWALL STEPS AND RAMPS TO THE BEACH CAN BE SLIPPERY WHEN WET, COVERED WITH SEAWEED OR ALGAE. TIDAL ACTION MAY DAMAGE PARTS OF THE WALKWAY AND ALTER THE LEVEL OF SAND BELOW THE STEPS.

PLEASE TAKE CARE WHEN WALKING ALONG THE SEAWALL AND USING THE STEPS AND RAMPS

Network Rail

Right: *In the days of Dawlish's 'down' colour light distant signal being positioned just in advance of the Rockstone Bridge, 'Western' Class 52 No. D1048 Western Lady traverses the Sea Wall on 31 May 1975 with the 09.50 Paddington to Newquay through service. Newquay, served by the single line from Par, still sees through services from London in the 2008 timetable with an FGW HST forming a daily return service, which is now (wrongly) marketed under the "Atlantic Coast Express" title.* **Norman E. Preedy**

Above: *Viewed from the Coastguard Footbridge at the London end of Dawlish Station, preserved GW 'King' No. 6024 King Edward I travels along the Sea Wall from Langstone and under the Rockstone footbridge with the southbound 'Torbay Express' from Bristol Temple Meads to Kingswear on 3 September 2006. The train is formed of a rather motley collection of different liveried Mk.1 stock.* **Author**

Left Above: *The original Coastguard lookout building has not been used for its intended purpose for many years and has recently been used as a restaurant and bar; however this business closed down in 2006 and the building is to be converted to residential use. With the original boat house on the left and the Coastguard's building on the right, First TransPennine-liveried Class 158 No. 158762 pulls away from its Dawlish stop on 12 August 2006 forming the 10.22 Paignton to Exmouth service.* **Author**

Left Below: *The Coastguard footbridge offers an excellent view of Dawlish station. In recent years a Network Rail engineering depot has been built at the Exeter end of the station car park and looks rather messy. When looking at this view it is hard to believe that until the late 1960s the car park was a thriving goods yard, collecting much local produce and transporting it to market, including crops as well as animals. Taken on 12 August 2006, a First Great Western HST set, led by power car No. 43170 with No. 43150 on the rear departs the station forming the 06.39 Penzance to Paddington.* **Author**

Right: *Freight traffic along the Sea Wall is hugely reduced these days when compared with the scene in the 1960s and 1970s. 30-40 years ago on average 15 freights were recorded every day working both up and down along the Sea Wall, with the author's own records showing that on 7 July 1974 a staggering eight freights went through the station between 17.00 and 20.00. Today freight traffic is down to just one or two per day. In much happier times, green-liveried Brush Type 4s (Class 47), No. 1906 is seen approaching Coastguard's Bridge leading train 7B33, the 11.55 Exeter Riverside to Truro freight, on 5 August 1971. At this time a cross-over was still in use between up and down tracks at the London end of Dawlish station.* **David Wharton**

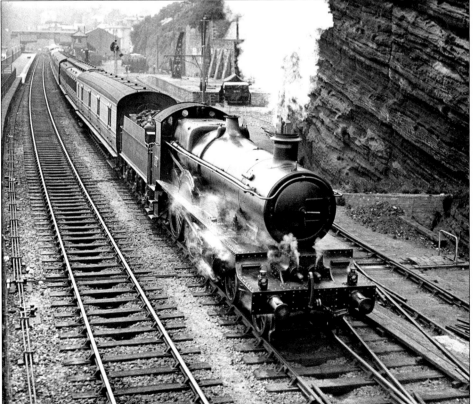

Above: *With evidence of major wooden platform damage on the 'down' side, sustained two years earlier in a storm which ripped up the platform decking, 'Western' Class 52 No. D1005* Western Venturer *passes through the platform at Dawlish with an empty stock move from Newton Abbot to Exeter St Davids on 21 June 1975. By this time the goods yard clearly visible in the black and white view below had gone and the area set out for car parking.* **Norman E. Preedy**

Left: *The same view looking over Dawlish station from the Coastguard's Bridge, this time taken in 1926. The goods yard is in full operation with a crane and loading platform. Departing on the 'up' is June 1914-built GW 'Star' class 4-6-0 No. 4054* Princess Charlotte *powering a London bound express. This loco was from the Plymouth allocation and a frequent visitor to the Sea Wall. It was withdrawn in February 1952.*
Bernard Whicher/Rail Archive Stephenson

Top: *The main entrance to Dawlish Station from Richmond Place is best described as 'uninspiring'. A cafe now occupies most of the ground floor and the view from the street of the station is dominated by an unpainted and tatty footbridge.* **Author**

Above Left: *An over domination of signage is attached to the station frontage advising of length limits in the car park, the name of the station, and notices to tell you to not to trespass or smoke on railway property, plus another framed 'Welcome to Dawlish' sign. The rather pleasing inset cast post box is almost lost.* **Author**

Above Right: *Viewed from the down platform, Freightliner Heavy Haul No. 66625 passes the station running light from Newton Abbot to Exeter on 22 June 2008. Note the present concrete and perspex roof.* **Author**

Right: *A view from Coastguard's Bridge showing the station, yard and goods shed in June 1926.* **Author's Collection**

Above:
To mark the Brunel 200 Anniversary, Dawlish Community Trust, with funding from the Heritage Lottery Fund, erected Dawlish Brunel Trail boards at five points between Lea Mount and Dawlish Warren. The board from the Viaduct, Dawlish is shown. **Author**

Top: *South West Trains Class 159 sets Nos. 159007 and 159015 slow for the Dawlish stop on 14 July 2002 forming the Sunday only 09.03 Waterloo to Plymouth service. The derelict signalbox can be seen on the left.* **Author**

Above and Left: *Dawlish signal box, located on the up platform opened on 9 September 1920 and closed on 5 October 1986 as part of the West of England re-signalling project. The box was an unusual style in having a vaulted upper storey, allowing the maximum through way on the platform. After closure the box was retained with the intention of letting out the structure for retail use. However countless attempts at this have failed. The structure has now fallen into serious disrepair and is covered in plastic sheeting to avoid bits falling off onto passing trains or the public. The box is now a listed structure. The view above shows the box when in use in the late 1970s, while the view left shows its 2008 condition. Both:* **Author**

Above: *Virgin Trains-operated Class 47 No. 47841* Spirit of Chester *emerges from the 209 yard long Kennaway tunnel into the daylight at Dawlish and starts to run parallel with Marine Parade towards Dawlish station, forming the 09.35 Penzance to Manchester Piccadilly on 14 July 2002. This rather unusual view of Dawlish is taken from the open section of the station footbridge using a 200mm lens. Note the headboard carried on the loco 'Brush Type 4 Fund' - this and several other headboards found their way onto many trains during the last year of regular Class 47 workings.* **Author**

Below: *A superb period view of a Birmingham RC&W three-car DMMU, slowing for the station stop at Dawlish on 29 June 1960 forming the 15.05 Exeter St Davids to Kingswear service. The set is painted in as-delivered BR green off-set by yellow whisker ends and a white cab roof. The three-car multiple units were just being introduced at this time on local services, replacing steam powered formations. In the West Country at the time considerable media hype surrounded the introduction of these 'new' trains complete with a toilet in the middle vehicle.* **Mike Mensing**

Top Left: *In the early years of the 21st Century Teignbridge Council erected several beach notices along the sea wall, advising tourists of the position of amenities with a panel for the high tide table, but in 2008 this was seldom kept up to date.* **Author**

Top Right: *The view of an 'up' train approaching Dawlish station, taken from the west end of the 'down' platform is always quite pleasing, even with modern lineside furniture and fencing in the way. On 22 June 2008, the 10.50 Plymouth to Paddington approaches the station led by power car No. 43091.* **Author**

Above: *Until 2007 when new tall black steel fencing was erected along the side of Marine Parade on the brick base of the railway right of way, photography over the original fence was easy, now a step ladder is required to see over the top. With another photographer recording the scene, Voyager Nos. 221116 with 221143 behind out of view pass Dawlish station on 7 August 2004 forming the 10.25 Newcastle to Penzance service.* **Author**

Left: *One of the landmarks at Dawlish for many years was the 'down' semaphore signal located on the land side of the 'up' line by the Colonnade Viaduct so positioned to aid drivers' sighting of the signal. In April 1960, GW 51xx class 2-6-2T No. 4136 pulls away from Dawlish with an Exeter to Kingswear service.* **J. C. Beckett**

Above: *After the demise of the Type 2 diesel-hydraulic locos in the west, BR standard Sulzer Type 2s of Class 25 arrived, which operated alongside Brush Type 2 Class 31s on stopping passenger and freight services. On 30 May 1976 Class 25/1 No. 25080, with the original body design having side louvres, pulls away from Dawlish with an evening Exeter St Davids to Newton Abbot service.* **Author**

Below: *If this and the above view are compared, little has noticeably changed in a span of 50 years. In this mid-1926 view GW 'Star' class 4-6-0 No. 4012 Knight of the Thistle departs from Dawlish with a semi-fast service for Plymouth. No. 4012 was built at Swindon in March 1908 and allocated to Plymouth, remaining in the west and finishing its days at Newton Abbot in 1949, just after the Nationalisation of the UK railways.* **Bernard Whicher/Rail Archive Stephenson**

Above and Below: *Another fascinating through the years comparison picture is this, showing the view of Dawlish station from the Sea Wall footpath on the sea side between Dawlish station and Kennaway Tunnel. This path offers exceptional views of the line, even if a short step ladder is needed to gain elevation. In the above view Southern Bulleid 'Battle-of-Britain light Pacific No. 34066* Spitfire *pulls out of Dawlish station in 1955 powering an Exeter St Davids to Plymouth stopping service. The view below, recorded on 31 July 2004 shows Virgin Trains 'Super Voyage' No. 221128* Captain John Smith *passing the station forming the 06.42 Summer Saturday Birmingham New Street to Paignton service. The station building and residential property has changed little over the years. The sea front ice cream cafe has been replaced with a more sturdy structure and a Beach Managers office has appeared on the 'up' side. In terms of track changes, the crossing from 'up' to 'down' line has now been removed.* **Bernard Whicher/Rail Archive Stephenson/Author**

Above and Below: *Ever since the standard gauge railway was opened along the front at Dawlish a footbridge has been located adjacent to the portal of Kennaway Tunnel, providing access from the Lea Mount footpath to the Sea Wall at Boat Cove. The original iron footbridge is seen in the upper view, showing the 'Torbay Express', emerging from the tunnel powered by GW 'Castle' No. 7001* Sir James Milne *(originally* Denbigh Castle*). On the 'down' line by the signal is a west bound pick-up freight heading for Kingswear. In the view below a rather unusual formation is seen in the same location in more modern times, with the 1960s built concrete and steel footbridge and modernised housing on the landward side. The train, captured on 13 June 2005, consists of Freightliner Heavy Haul Class 47 No. 47150 hauling former DRS No. 20905, rail-blue-liveried No. 20096, and 'Deltic' No. 55019 en route from the South Devon Railway at Totnes to Barrow Hill following a Diesel Gala exhibition on the Totnes to Buckfastleigh line.* **T. G. Hepburn/Rail Archive Stephenson/Author**

Film Strip: **1.** *EWS Class 37s pass along the Sea Wall at Dawlish with a Rail Head Treatment Train.* **2.** *Network Rail-liveried Class 31 traverses the Sea Wall by Kennaway Tunnel during a driver training programme.* **3.** *Probably the most odd liveried HST power car ever No. 43087 painted in Hornby red and yellow livery hauling buffet car No. 40810 and Cotswold Rail-liveried power car No. 43070 forming a Laira bound stock move - this was the last ever run of the Hornby-liveried powercar.* All: **Author**

Main Picture: *From their introduction until 2007 Class 158s were a common sight on the Dawlish Sea Wall, but reallocations and changed routes now means few class members work west of Exeter. Painted in Central Trains green livery, set No. 158795 departs from Dawlish on the down on 1 July 2006 forming the 13.00 Cardiff to Paignton service.* **Author**

Above: *Lea Mount, on the west side of Dawlish, offers the most outstanding views of Lyme Bay, with on a good day, Portland being easily visible from the upper levels. In terms of the railway it offers a huge variety of different views of 'down' trains all the way from Langstone Rock to the approaches to Kennaway Tunnel. BR blue-liveried 'Western' No. D1040* Western Queen *hurries towards Kennaway Tunnel on 14 June 1973 with a Paignton-bound express from Paddington. If this and later views from the same location are compared the general housing growth of Dawlish's east side is very noticeable, with such local landmarks as the Grand Hotel, Lanhern House and the Charlton House Hotel all replaced by new structures.* **Author**

Right Middle: *A very rare visitor to the Dawlish Sea Wall on a revenue earning train was Class 59/1 No. 59101* Village of Whatley *on 5 September 1998 when it powered a rake of aggregate box wagons from Whatley Quarry to Goodrington sidings for Flexia Construction, who at the time were engaged in cable TV installation in the area. The stone was to be used for 'make good' work on paths and roads. With a little help from the train operators, the sole revised liveried ARC loco was used for this duty.* **Author**

Right Bottom: *Another rare visitor to the Sea Wall was EWS VIP loco No. 67029, painted in silver livery with large bodyside 'animal head' logos. The loco is usually used to power the EWS managers' train and is occasionally used for charter work. On 21 May 2005 the loco is seen between Dawlish Station and Kennaway Tunnel powering the 06.50 Swansea to Penzance 'The Eden Belle' Pathfinder charter.* **Author**

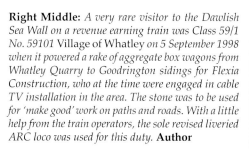

Above: *A panoramic 'stitched' picture of Dawlish from the end of Dawlish breakwater. On the left is Parsons Tunnel and the far right Langstone.* **Kevin Wills**

Main Picture: *The entire Dawlish front, viewed from Lea Mount, showing a 'down' Class 221 and an 'up' FGW HST traversing the wall.* **Author**

Above: *In the period after First Group was re-awarded the Great Western Franchise in April 2006 a major refurbishment policy was drawn up for both HST power cars and trailer stock. Power cars Nos. 43004 and 43009 and three coaches were repainted into an early 'dynamic lines' livery, the only power cars so treated. Fully branded No. 43009* First Transforming Travel *heads towards Kennaway Tunnel on 15 July 2006 leading the 07.35 Paddington to Penzance service. Note the rough sea for mid-summer.* **Author**

Left Middle: *In the days when Dawlish was a very popular seaside resort, with hundreds of people on the beach and no fewer than 20 concrete and wood seats on the Sea Wall to sit and enjoy the view of the bay, a green-liveried 'Warship' heads west on 25 July 1962. The car parking in the adjacent Marine Parade was at this time angular, then for a period it became normal curb parking, before recent council changes have re-introduced angled parking in a quest to cram more vehicles in the town's limited parking.*
A. P. Crane

Left Bottom: *From the December 2008 timetable change, Arriva Cross Country commenced using four fully refurbished HST sets on some long distance north east - south west services, increasing the passenger loadings and providing a more pleasing travelling environment. With power cars refurbished by Brush Traction and passenger stock by Wabtec of Doncaster, the trains all sport the new silver, brown and pink corporate livery. On 17 December 2008, the 06.00 Leeds to Plymouth passes Dawlish formed of six trailer vehicles led by power car No. 43301. On the rear was power car No. 43384. This view was recorded from the edge of the footbridge crossing the line by Kennaway Tunnel.* **Author**

Above: *A low level view taken from the end of Marine Parade, looking down the straight of the line towards Dawlish station on 21 September 1948, just nine months after the UK railways were nationalised, shows GW 28xx class 2-8-0 freight loco No. 2857 powering west with a heavy freight. No. 2857 was built by the Great Western Railway at Swindon in 1918. After withdrawal from BR in 1963, No. 2857 was sent to a Barry scrapyard where it remained until 1974 when it was saved from disposal. It is now owned by the 2857 Society and kept on the Severn Valley Railway.* **P. C. Short**

Right: *From the mid-afternoon onwards until the sun sets, a well illuminated view of a 'down' train approaching Kennaway Tunnel is possible from the land side by the footbridge crossing the entrance of the tunnel. It is possible to get the beach, much of the Sea Wall, Langstone rock and even the Exmouth-Sidmouth coast line in the picture. During their brief period of operation west of Exeter on staff training duties, FGW Class 180 sets Nos. 180107 and 180101 head towards Kennaway Tunnel on 5 August 2004 forming the 14.35 Paddington to Plymouth service.* **Author**

Above: *The section of line through the five tunnels between Dawlish and Teignmouth remained single track until between 1902-05 due to the amount of structural work required to increase the size of the tunnels and cut back surrounding hills to provide clearance for double track operation. With wheeled beach huts on the foreshore, this superb picture dated 1901 shows Great Western Railway 'Atbara' class 4-4-0 No. 3388* Sir Redvers *pulling out of the western portal of Kennaway Tunnel with an express bound for Plymouth.* **Dr Tice F. Budden/Rail Archive Stephenson**

Left: *The gardens above Kennaway Tunnel, Lea Mount, offer an excellent view of trains passing around the headland between Dawlish and Teignmouth. This view taken from the top of the gardens shows an up HST emerging from the 224 yard long Coryton Tunnel and paralleling Coryton Beach as it heads towards Kennaway Tunnel on 3 October 1980. In the distance on the left is Parson head and Parsons Tunnel.* **Author**

Above: *In recent years the foliage between the Dawlish-Teignmouth tunnels has been allowed to grow to unprecedented levels, frequently causing earth slips. The area between Kennaway and Coryton Tunnels once housed allotments on the landward side, but now it is just a mass of trees and bushes. Emerging from Coryton Tunnel on 22 July 2006, Virgin Trains' 'hire-in' GNER HST set working the 10.32 Paignton to Newcastle Summer Saturday service led by power car No. 43111, takes a train load of holiday makers home.* **Author**

Below: *With the town of Dawlish and its station on the right, this is the view between Clerks and Parsons Tunnels. Taken on 14 February 1989, Class 108 DMMU set No. P955 forms the 06.45 Swindon to Penzance service, rather a long way to travel in a first generation DMU.* **Author**

Above: *One of the better known locations for photography between the Sea Wall tunnels is Horse Cove, where a public footpath from Old Teignmouth Road crosses the fields and at its lowest level gives a view of trains emerging from the 66yd long Clerks tunnel. With Dawlish in the background and the sun out, this is a superb view of the bay. In terms of light, early afternoon provides the best illumination. An InterCity 'Swallow' liveried HST is seen heading west on 23 June 1994, forming the 11.35 Paddington to Penzance, led by power car No. 43187.* **Author**

Left: *Seldom do we see pictures of 'up' trains in the Horse Cove, Clerks Tunnel area, as compared with the view looking towards Dawlish it is fairly plain. On 7 June 1988, No. 43193 Yorkshire Post heads towards Clerks Tunnel and under the bi-directional signal with the 14.05 Paignton to Newcastle service. As was standard with Cross Country formations only one first class carriage was provided.* **Author**

Above: *Compared to the view left, the scene has not changed much at Horse Cove in over 50 years, with less lineside growth and fewer buildings on the horizon. GW 'Castle' 4-6-0 No. 5049* Earl of Plymouth *heads west on a splendid photographic summer afternoon in the 1950s. This loco, built in April 1936, was named* Denbigh Castle *for its first 16 months before renaming. Many of today's railway followers think renamings are a thing of the present era, but dozens of Great Western locos were renamed over the years.* **Peter Gray**

Below: *Between 2005-07 Gloucester-based Cotswold Rail held a contract to pilot First Great Western internal stock moves if required. One of these was on 18 April 2007 when Class 47 No. 47810* Captain Sensible *powered a special 13.14 Bristol Stoke Gifford to Laira HST stock move, following a fatality involving the set the previous day. The train is seen emerging from Clerke Tunnel and passing low tide at Horse Cove.* **Author**

IT'S CARNIVAL TIME IN DAWLISH

The third week of August is Dawlish Carnival Week. The first event was in 1968 and since then the event has greatly increased in size and for the several years has included a spectacular Carnival Air Show in the skies above the railway and beach during the actual carnival day (Thursday) afternoon.

Apart from the usual carnival style events and street procession, the air show attracts a massive following from outside the area with some people travelling from Europe to witness the flying displays, which usually include such attractions as the RAF Aerobatic Display Team, The Red Arrows, helicopter flying, private owner aircraft displays and often the Battle of Britain Memorial Flight including the Lancaster, Spitfire and Hurricane.

In terms of the railway, the event brings huge extra patronage and in some years extra trains have been organised to operate between Exeter St Davids and Newton Abbot. In 2006 this consisted of a First Great Western Class 180 providing a 'shuttle' service. In 2007 the extra trains had to be cancelled at the last minute due to safety case issues of FGW operating 'top and tailed' Class 67s with Mk2 stock, but for the 2008 event these problems were resolved.

The Sea Wall, bridges, beach and Lea Mount form the main observation areas for the Carnival Air Show.

The town of Dawlish, and especially the Carnival Committee pray all year for good weather on the event day and usually the town is lucky; in the past 40 years very few events have had to be called off. ∎

Far Left Above: *People start to gather for the Dawlish Carnival Air Show many hours before the show. With the beach full and few spaces left on the Sea Wall. Hired-in Centro Class 150/1 No. 150102 pulls away from Dawlish on 14 August 2003 with an additional Wessex Trains service from Exeter to Newton Abbot.* **Author**

Left Top: *What most people come to see - the stunning RAF Red Arrow's, with all nine aircraft coming straight for Dawlish above a pleasure craft from Exmouth during the 2007 event.* **Author**

Left Bottom: *How the pilots see the Dawlish Carnival and also a very unusual view of Dawlish station and sea front. Taken during the 2006 Carnival on 17 August, four Gazelle helicopters from the Blue Eagles display team fly past Dawlish, the view was taken from another helicopter of the same flight.* **Kevin Wills**

Above: *With little room left on the Sea Wall or beach, crowds gather for the 2007 Dawlish Carnival Air Show, as an FGW HST pulls away from the station after having made an extra stop with a 'down' Paddington to Plymouth service to cater for the crowds.* **Author**

Right Middle: *For the 2008 Carnival, First Great Western operated loco-hauled relief services between Exeter and Newton Abbot, formed of five coaches top and tailed by Class 67s Nos. 67021 and 67022. An afternoon westbound departure is seen leaving Dawlish.* **Author**

Right Bottom: *For the 2008 Dawlish Air Show, air display organiser Kevin Wills arranged for a stunning RAF 'Role Display' featuring a Boeing E-3D Sentry AEW1 'AWACS', four Tornado fighters and two RAF Hawks. E-3D Sentry No. ZH07 is shown above a pair of Tornado GR4 aircraft passing low over Dawlish.* **Author**

THE SEA WALL AND INCLEMENT WEATHER

Inclement weather and rough seas have taken their toll on the Dawlish Sea Wall ever since the line was constructed. Serious wash outs occurred in the Shell Cove area in 1880 which required expensive remedial action and closure of the line for eight days. In the early years of the 20th Century numerous wash-outs were recorded in and around Dawlish station. In 1908 several hundred yards of the wall between Dawlish station and the Coastguard's Bridge was washed away.

In more recent times, serious storms in 1962-63 washed away a significant section of the wall and footpath near the Rockstone bridge and virtually the entire length between Dawlish Station and Kennaway Tunnel, with the wrought iron fencing destroyed, ballast washed away and the tracks buckled.

Most years the railway has received serious damage and few have passed without some form of closure while repairs are carried out. The Sea Wall is a constant maintenance nightmare and has been ever since it was built, with two tides every day little time exists for major repairs to be undertaken or safeguarding work carried out.

Numerous calls have been made to even abandon the route in favour of an inland route which would not face such ravages of the weather; however such drastic action is unlikely to happen in the foreseeable future.

The areas most susceptible to damage are between the station and Kennaway Tunnel and on the main wall around Rockstone Bridge. The continuation of the wall around to Coryton Beach is also frequently damaged and the beach huts destroyed or even tossed onto the line.

The area around Cockwood Harbour and Powderham, even on the River Exe, get a buffeting from the high water and it is not unknown to have small boats, or masts from boats, land on the line.

The weather problems are not always confined to the winter months and in June 2008 a major hole was found under the wall close to Dawlish Station which had to receive emergency repairs. ∎

Above: *After introduction, the Class 220 and 221 'Voyager' sets were a major problem when passing along the Sea Wall in rough weather conditions, for water ingress into roof electrical equipment caused electrical systems to shut down and the sets fail, requiring assistance. Set No. 221120 passes Dawlish forming the 07.35 Bristol to Paignton on 9 September 2006.* **Author**

Left: *The Dawlish Sea Wall gets a summer pounding on 15 July 2006, the force of impact on this day causing some minor structural damage. However, people are still to be seen risking their lives trying to walk on the footpath.* **Author**

Film Strip Below: 1. *The wall is impacted on 12 October 1999.* **2**. *Debris is strewn on the tracks after a storm on 28 October 2004 which closed the line for three days.* **3**. *The remains of beach huts which were once located behind wall defences by Coryton Cove.* **4**. *Engineers use a road/rail vehicle to repair damage to the tracks and fabric of Dawlish station following the October 2004 storm. All:* **Author**

Above: *On 21 September 2006, Network Rail was keeping a minute by minute watch on the Sea Wall with a higher than average tide and a strong South West wind. This picture of set No. 150253 forming the 17.54 Exmouth to Paignton was taken at 18.50 and was the last 'down' train allowed through on its correct line. After this, until 22.00, single line working over the 'up' bi-directional line was introduced.* **Author**

Right: *With wash-out boards pulled out from the track centre and huge amounts of ballast washed away or thrown into the adjacent Marine Parade, this was the scene faced by the Network Rail clean up crews on 28 October 2008 after one of the fiercest storm to hit the wall for several years.* **Author**

Film Strip Below: **1**. *The sea hammers the section of wall between the station and Kennaway Tunnel.* **2**. *With waves higher than the station on 21 September 2006 serious damage was caused to many sections.* **3**. *Network Rail and private contractors get to work on 29 October 2004 to clear up damage.* **4**. *The Sea Wall path is re-cemented after a storm in October 1989.* *All:* **Author**

TEIGNMOUTH SEA WALL TO TEIGNMOUTH DOCKS

After emerging from the 512 yard long Parsons Tunnel the railway line hugs the Teignmouth Sea Wall through to Teignmouth station. The line was opened on 30 May 1846 by the South Devon Railway.

As the railway approaches Teignmouth, the line bears away from the sea. Originally a tunnel, known as Eastcliffe Tunnel, existed at this point, but it was opened-out in 1884 to allow for station expansion and the laying of double track. Between opening and 1884 a loop line was provided on the Teignmouth Sea Wall section. A tunnel also existed at the west end of Teignmouth station but this was removed in 1881.

At the same time as Eastcliffe Tunnel was removed, the iconic 'Skew Bridge' which dominates all pictures taken at the east end of Teignmouth was opened.

Teignmouth station was originally the terminus of the line from Exeter, becoming a through station when the line was extended to Newton Abbot from 17 December 1847. Originally it was operated by the atmospheric system but by September the following year this had been abandoned and normal steam operation introduced.

For the first two years of life, Teignmouth station had just a single platform, but traffic levels soon required additional facilities.

In keeping with the rest of the Sea Wall route, broad gauge track was replaced with standard gauge on 20 May 1892 and between then and 1895 the station was totally rebuilt, with an opulent, quite large station, much in keeping with other major west Country holiday towns such as Weston-super-Mare and Torquay. Much of the station building remains today.

Such was the growth of passenger traffic at Teignmouth and the number of holiday trains using the station, that by 1938 the 'down' platform had been extended to accommodate up to 15 coach trains.

Teignmouth had a small goods yard, located on the 'up' side with a very tight entrance at the Exeter end of the 'up' platform. General freight traffic was handled by the station until 14 June 1965 and coal traffic until the end of 1967 when all facilities were closed. Today the former goods yard is the site of industrial units.

Signalling at Teignmouth was controlled by a small manual signalbox with 31 levers, located at the west end of the 'down' platform, opened in 1896 to replace an original structure. Teignmouth signal box was closed on 15 November 1986 as part of the West of England modernisation with control passing to Exeter panel box.

Heading west from Teignmouth trains go through a brick and stone face cutting, passing through residential areas until Teignmouth Docks are reached, operated today by Associated British Ports (ABP). The port was rail connected until 1969 and had its own signalbox, Teignmouth Old Quay. After passing Teignmouth Dock, the line now skirting the River Teign heads towards Shaldon bridge.

Directly at the west end of Teignmouth station is a facing crossing from the 'up' to 'down' line this is a signalled crossover for trains heading west on the bi-directional track from Dawlish Warren, and sees use during periods of inclement weather. ■

Below: *Another view which has hardly changed in more than 100 years. This was the view of a 'down' stopping service emerging from Parsons Tunnel, Teignmouth in 1908. The train is powered by a Great Western 3031 class 4-2-2 'Dean Single' No. 3030* Westward Ho. *At this point a footpath leads down to the railway and beach from the main Teignmouth to Dawlish road by the village of Holcombe and is thus the start of the Teignmouth Sea Wall section.*
Robert Brookman/Rail Archive Stephenson

Above: *The view of Parsons Tunnel in the modern era. With extra sea defences now built up around the portal of Parsons Tunnel to reduce the risk of wash outs, a First Great Western HST set with powercar No. 43148 leading pulls out of the tunnel on 6 April 2002 forming the 08.45 Paddington to Plymouth service. At this time the train was painted in 'fag-packet' green livery while the power car was in the first version of the First Group blue and white 'swirl' colours.* **Author**

Right: *It is rare to find photographs taken of 'down' trains from the land side at Parsons Tunnel, but this superb view taken in the mid-1950s has been found showing Great Western 7200 class 2-8-2T No. 7220 powering a westbound general merchandise freight. The 7200 class were one of the largest tank engines to operate in the UK and were rebuilds of 2-8-0Ts in 1934-39 with a total fleet size of 54. The locos had a power classification of 8F and weighed just over 92 tons.* **E. D. Bruton**

Above & Below: *The view looking west from the area around Parsons Tunnel has changed little over the years, with the rock face, wall and sea shore still virtually the same. Track relaying has been done with the use of concrete sleepers replacing wood and continuous welded rail has replaced 60ft bull-head track. In the upper view, EWS Class 66/0 No. 66189 approaches Parsons Tunnel on 6 April 2002 leading the Saturdays only 08.33 Burngullow to Crewe china clay service. The tanks on the train were bound for Caledonian Paper Mills at Irvine in Scotland. In the lower view, GW 'King' No. 6025* King Henry III *makes light work of the 10-car formation on the 09.45 Newquay to Paddington on 18 June 1959.* **Author/K. L. Cook/Rail Archive Stephenson**

Right: *With what appears to be a small embankment fire above, which might well have been caused by the passing of a previous steam train, Swindon-built 'Warship' No. D804* Avenger*, prior to modification to carry a four position route indicator panel, passes along the Teignmouth Sea Wall on 18 June 1959. The loco is powering the 07.30 Penzance to Manchester cross country service which at the time also conveyed a portion from Kingswear to Manchester, attached at Newton Abbot and detached in Birmingham.*
Mike Mensing

Left: *On Wednesday 8 April 1964 Western Region history was made when 'Western' No. D1027* Western Lancer *powered a 250 ton 'speed trial' between Paddington and Plymouth setting up a new 3 hour record. Even today with HSTs this is hard to beat with the fastest in 2008 between Plymouth and Paddington still being 3 hours on the 06.00 departure from Plymouth, but the schedule is seldom met! The historic 1964 run is seen between Sprey Point and Teignmouth, running under clear signals. The loco is painted in BR Western Region maroon livery, off-set by a small yellow warning end.* **John Clarke**

Right: *The Beyer-Peacock 'Hymek' Type 3 diesel-hydraulic locos were never that common in the West Country; however on some Summer Saturdays class members did operate on some workings. On 4 August 1962, all-over BR green-liveried No. D7006 pulls away from Teignmouth and past Sprey Point with a holiday relief from Kingswear to Wolverhampton.*
John K. Morton

Main Picture: *From the mid-way point along the Teignmouth Sea Wall at Sprey Point a superb view exists looking towards Teignmouth. The sea front properties of the town and St Michaels church dominate the distant view with some of the higher properties of Shaldon on the distant hills. On 5 July 1984, Class 47 No. 47510 Fair Rosamund approaches Sprey Point powering the 07.00 Plymouth to Newcastle service in place of the booked HST set.* **Inset:** *Again the 'modern' view has not altered largely. Some rock protection fencing has been erected and mesh placed on the hill, but otherwise the view is very similar. On 28 August 2004 'Super Voyager' No. 221122 passes the same spot forming the 08.25 Plymouth to Edinburgh CrossCountry service. Both:* **Author.**

Above & Left: *The 1884 'Skew Bridge' over the line directly at the Exeter end of Teignmouth station is an icon of the area, appearing in virtually every picture taken on the Teignmouth end of the Sea Wall. The view has changed little in the last 125 years apart from removal of the semaphore signals and extra growth on the embankments. In the view above shows Great Western Railway 'Badminton' class 4-4-0 No. 3294 Blenheim with a superb rake of period GW stock departing from Teignmouth in 1903 on a local service. The 'Badminton' class was first introduced in 1897 by Dean. No. 3294 became No. 4102 in the GW 1912 renumbering. The view left shows BR Standard Class 9F 2-10-0 No. 92206 pulling around the curve away from Teignmouth on 26 June 1959 with an up freight from Plymouth.* **Robert Brookman Rail Archive Stephenson / Stan Creer**

Right & Below: *The semaphore signal on the down line was repositioned further towards Sprey Point in the mid-1960s and removed completely in the mid 1980s with West of England re-signalling. Taken on 5 July 1984, Class 47/0 No. 47146 rounds the Teignmouth curve and under Skew Bridge powering the 06.15 Plymouth to Paddington vans. On the left the main promenade can be seen with the Parish church of St Michaels with its square tower above. Below we see First/GBRf Class 66/7 No. 66724 in the same location on 23 May 2007 hauling a rake of First Great Western Mk.3 HST stock to Bombardier Derby Works for refurbishment. Throughout 2007 a constant movement of FGW stock along the Sea Wall was seen in conjunction with the fleet refurbishment, with in some weeks up to three transit moves recorded. Most of these workings were in the hands of Bristol-based GBRf drivers who frequently attached their 'Bristol Bluebirds' headboard. Both:* **Author**

Main Picture: *The view from the sea end of the Skew Bridge offers this superb vista of the Teignmouth Sea Wall, with the portal of Parsons Tunnel visible in the left background. The train shown is the 10.05 Paddington to Penzance on 11 August 2007 led by refurbished and MTU-fitted powercar No. 43165.* **Inset:** *In the era of 'Peak' power on the sea wall, Class 45 No. D138 rounds the curve at Teignmouth taken from the bridge embankment on 14 August 1971 powering the 09.25 Derby to Penzance.* **Author/Norman E. Preedy**

Main Picture: *The bridge linking the town's car park with the sea front offers an excellent view of 'up' trains passing through or departing from Teignmouth station, with the disused Exeter end section of the 'down' platform clearly visible with ivy encrusted lamp posts. On 3 July 2008, Arriva Trains Cross Country liveried 'Voyager' No. 220026 pulls away from the station stop with the 10.04 Paignton to Newcastle service.*
Inset: *On 4 June 1960 a three-car BRCW 'suburban' DMMU departs the station with a Kingswear to Exeter local.*
Author/Les Elsey

Above: *Receiving a little attention from its driver during station dwell time, 'Dean Single' or Great Western 3031 class No. 3032* Agamemnon *awaits to depart from Teignmouth in 1903 with an 'up' London express.* Agamemnon *was built at Swindon in July 1894 and withdrawn in October 1913.* **Robert Brookman/ Rail Archive Stephenson**

Below: *Taken from mid-way along the 'down' platform at Teignmouth on 21 September 1948, just nine months after Nationalisation of the UK railways, Ministry of Supply 2-8-0 No. 79235 heads an 'up' freight. The bridge under which the train is passing has been replaced in recent years with a brick structure, while the points which the loco is about to pass gave access to the small Teignmouth goods yard and have now been removed.* **P. C. Short**

Above: *Teignmouth signal box, located at the country end of the down platform, was built in 1896 and had 31 levers. It interfaced with Parsons Tunnel in the east until 1964 and then Dawlish, while westward it interfaced with Bishopsteignton and then Newton Abbot. In keeping with all boxes of the era they were kept in pristine condition by staff and by looking at the equipment shelf in this June 1949 view, Teignmouth was no exception. Teignmouth box was a 24 hour operation and closed on 15 November 1986 as part of the West of England re-signalling.* **E. D. Bruton**

Above: *The present Teignmouth station was opened in 1895 and was a substantial structure in keeping with other major facilities at principal holiday resorts such as Weston-super-Mare and Torquay. The main buildings are located on the 'down' side with a footbridge linking to the 'up' platform. Today much of the structure is let to retail businesses but the railway still operate a sizeable ticket and information office and has offices on the platform. Viewed from the 1970s modernised car park, this view was recorded in June 2008.* **Author**

Below: *Looking over Teignmouth station at the west end from Shute Hill, this view shows a down First Great Western HST passing through the 'down' platform on 29 June 2008; the station footbridge can be seen mid-way along the platform. Both platforms still retain near full length canopies with original ironwork. The open land on the far left is the former Teignmouth goods yard, which was accessed from the far end. Teignmouth signalbox was located in the bottom right corner.* **Author**

Left: *The view from the road bridge linking Teignmouth with Shaldon and the coast road towards Torquay offers a good photographic and viewing location. With the children's playing park in the background, this 8 August 1956 view shows Great Western-design 'Modified Hall' No. 6990* Witherslack Hall *hauling two vans, a brake van and two passenger coaches towards Newton Abbot. No. 6990, built in March 1948, is now preserved on the Great Central Railway, Loughborough.* **Tom Williams**

Below: *With the playground now the local Rugby pitch and many new residential properties built in the area, this is the 2006 view from the same spot. Even though trackside fences have now been erected, these are not too obtrusive if carefully positioned in pictures. The train is the 08.55 Cardiff to Paignton formed of Class 153 'Bubble' No. 153373 painted in Bristol-Weymouth advertising livery and Class 150/2 No. 150253 painted in Wessex Trains route advertising colours. By 2009 all local multiple unit sets were repainted in the corporate colours of First Group and the vast majority had been fully refurbished internally.* **Author**

Above, Right & Below: *Looking west from Shaldon Bridge, this offers a pleasing view of trains rounding the curve by Teignmouth boat yard, with some interesting land formations on the Teign estuary. In the above view, BR Swindon-built 'Warship' No. D804* Avenger *rounds the headland powering the 'up' Torbay Express in 1959. The view right shows BR rail blue-liveried 'Western' No. D1042* Western Princess *leading the 08.35 Penzance to Paddington on 31 August 1971, while the view below shows hired-in Midland Mainline HST set with power car No. 43007 leading the 11.50 Plymouth to Newcastle on 5 April 2007. In the latter days of Virgin Trains operation of the CrossCountry franchise one HST set on weekdays and four on Summer Saturdays were hired to operate long distance services. Under the Arriva Cross Country franchise HSTs have been re-introduced on selected services.* **IA-L/Geoff Gillham/Author**

ENGINEERING WORK ALONG THE SEA WALL

Engineering work on the Sea Wall section tends to fall into two main categories, emergency repair work following wash outs or wall damage and planned track renewals and infrastructure replacement.

Planned track renewals are organised months in advance with carefully managed train movements working into the engineering sections just at the required time and in the correct order. These are complex operations and are normally undertaken at weekends when the line is closed to all normal services.

In recent years, major track renewals have been undertaken in the Powderham, Starcross, Cockwood, Dawlish, Teignmouth and Newton Abbot areas. Under the present privatised railway, track renewal trains for the Sea Wall area are operated by DB Schenker (previously EWS) from the engineering base at Westbury with anything from between four to ten trains arriving in convoy at the start of work, allowing the old track formation to be lifted out, old ballast removed, a new formation laid, tracks repositioned and the lines tamped and lined ready for service at line speed.

During the 2005-08 relaying operations, trains worked west through the work sites running round at either Newton Abbot or Goodrington (Paignton) before returning to Westbury.

During these major periods of work it is frequently required to operate trains in the 'wrong' direction to normal running.

Emergency track repairs are more complex. Usually these can be carried out without the need for heavy engineering trains and deal with small wash-outs of the under ballast or sea wall, however in major cases extra stone or boulders have been required and then a special short term planning train is operated, which could bring ballast, rock or mechanical plant into the area from Westbury and the Mendip aggregate sites or Meldon Quarry.

Some recent washouts required one or both lines to be closed for three or four days while ballast was replaced and thorough checks carried out to ensure no long term damage had been sustained.

Ongoing daily maintenance to the Sea Wall, in both the Dawlish and Teignmouth areas is carried out by private engineering firms outbased in the former yard at Dawlish, which are provided with special mechanical plant that can safely access the Sea Wall path from Dawlish Warren, Dawlish and Teignmouth and allow men to work at low tide times and with the walkways kept open to the public.

In periods of very rough sea, especially when a south westerly wind blows, the Sea Wall is placed on a constant guard by either Network Rail or a private engineering firm to ensure all is well. ∎

Film Strip: 1. *A special road vehicle based at Dawlish is used for repairs to the wall, here dealing with re-pointing work.* **2**. *A rail-mounted people mover is used to take staff to work sites, seen here at Dawlish Warren.* **3**. *Sleeper off-loading underway at Dawlish in 2007 in connection with re-laying the down line.* **4**. *Private engineers close off a small section of the Dawlish Sea Wall while repointing work is carried out on the wall face in 2008. All:* **Author**

Above: *For several weekends in November and December 2005 major engineering work took place around Dawlish and Teignmouth with significant sections of track renewed on both the up and down lines. On 18 December 2005 it was the turn of the up line between Kennaway Tunnel and Dawlish station platform to be replaced. The old track formation was removed overnight onto empty wagons which were then drawn forward to Teignmouth, while at first light new ballast and sleepers were lowered into position. Here a road/rail vehicle collects sleepers from a train stabled on the down line and carefully positions them at the correct spacing for the up line formation. The train is 'top and tailed' by EWS Class 60 No. 60025 and Class 59/2 No. 59202.* **Author**

Left: *On Sunday 20 November 2005 the down line was relaid in the area of Dawlish platform. Fresh ballast was brought to the worksite from Westbury by EWS Class 60 No. 60017* Shotton Steel Works *which is shown working down the 'up' line while a road/rail vehicle unloads the stone.* **Author**

Below: *On 24 April 1991, a section of the up line near to Kennaway Tunnel was relayed, and three works trains were in use. Illustrated here is Civil Engineers 'Dutch' liveried Class 37/0 No. 37254 standing on the up line adjacent to Marine Parade with a loaded 'Seacow' ballast train complete with a 'Shark' plough brake van on the rear, ready to run through the new track section and drop ballast.* **Author**

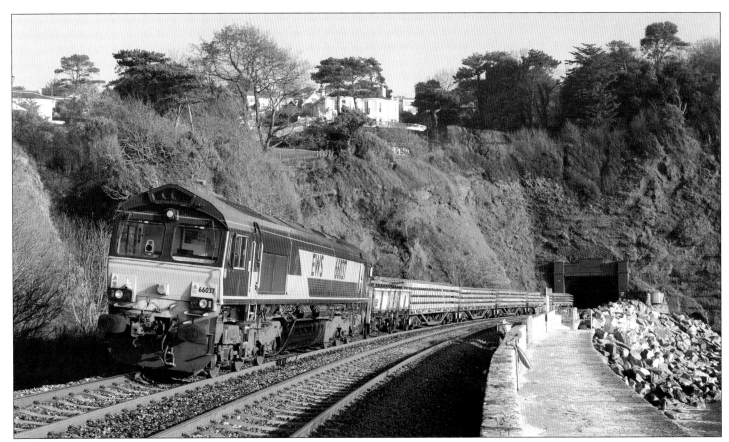

Above: *After removing old track panels from the Dawlish station area overnight on 10-11 December 2005, Class 66/0 No. 66037 was drawn forward to just the west side of Parsons Tunnel before being stabled for some 12 hours, while further work ahead prevented the train from going towards Newton Abbot and running round. The track panels are mounted four to a wagon on 'Salmon' bolster flats, they were removed to Westbury for recovery and disposal. Oil from the '66s' sump was dripping all day while stabled at Teignmouth, due to the angle of the loco on the canted track.* **Author**

Right: *Viewed from the Skew Bridge at Teignmouth, an entire procession of ballast trains was found stabled on Sunday 20 November 2005 while relaying was performed at Dawlish. In the foreground we see No. 66052 with track crane 78217 behind, after that is No. 66186 on a rake of bogie Network Rail ballast wagons loaded with spoil, while protruding from Parsons Tunnel No. 66006 can be seen with a spoil train.* **Author**

Below: *Ballast and relaying operations of an earlier generation. On 12 June 1967 BR Swindon-built 'Warship' No. D823 Hermes is seen carefully 'backing up' at Teignmouth propelling a short rake of ballast wagons, complete with engineering staff hitching a ride. The person in charge of the work is hanging out the side of the loco and not a single yellow vest can be seen.* **Geoff Gillham**

THE TEIGN ESTUARY TO NEWTON ABBOT

Forward from Shaldon Bridge the line follows the River Teign towards Bishopsteignton and Newton (the suffix Abbot not being added until 1877), it was opened on 30 December 1846 with the extension of the line from Teignmouth.

Heading west the line passes the village of Bishopsteignton, which has never had a station, before arriving at Newton Abbot passing Hackney yard, Newton Abbot race course and the site of the huge depot and workshops of the Great Western Railway and BR on the down side.

Just before Newton Abbot station was the junction with the Mortonhampstead line, which is now a closed freight only spur to Heathfield.

The original South Devon Railway station at Newton Abbot was in need of replacement and in the immediate pre First World War years plans were drawn up to build a large station. The original goods depot was moved to new premises on the Mortonhampstead Line, while sidings were laid on Hackney Marshes opening towards the end of 1911.

After World War I was over, the new Newton Abbot station was built, now facing the town and on to Queen Street. The building was formally opened on 11 April 1927. Adjacent to the station site was Newton Abbot works and depot, which was used extensively in the late 1800s to rebuild broad gauge vehicles to standard gauge and played an important role in rolling stock operations right up until the mid-1970s. The workshops, with a traverser, were responsible for heavy maintenance on diesel-hydraulic classes, while a significant carriage works existed at the west end of the site. Many sidings were located between the depot and station.

In modern traction days a diesel depot and carriage depot existed together with fuelling and service points.

The diesel depot closed in the mid-1970s and gradually fell into disrepair, being largely demolished in the 1990s and the site used for industrial units.

The branch to Mortonhampstead closed to passengers in February 1959, goods traffic was cut back to Bovey from April 1964 and further cut back to Heathfield from July 1970. The line is now mothballed.

The yard at Hackney does still see frequent traffic in terms of Freightliner Heavy Haul ballast services. Ballast trains from Burngullow in Cornwall split and stable in the yard several times each week. Until 2006 Cement trains also used the same method of operating due to restrictions on powering heavy trains over the arduous banks west of Newton Abbot.

Newton Abbot with its many lines, junctions and connections, had two large signal boxes from 1926/27 until re-signalling in 1987. Newton Abbot East had 206 levers while Newton Abbot West had 153 levers.

An intermediate signal box on this section existed at Bishopsteignton until 1969 and another at Hackney operated between 1891 and 1971.

In terms of photography, the section between Shaldon Bridge and Newton Abbot is the least accessible. A bridge does cross the line at Teignmouth Boat yard but recent fences restrict photography. A way under the line close to Bishopsteignton and a small footpath overbridge allow limited access, the former only at low tide. A couple of private over bridges also exist adjacent to campsites along the River Teign towards Newton Abbot. The shores of the river around Hackney Marshes can be accessed from a drive way at The Passage House Inn, with views of down trains possible. Photography at Newton Abbot station is good and an overbridge at the west end of the station gives a good vantage point. ■

Below: Taken from what is locally known as the River Teign 'Pill Box', this vantage point can only be reached at low tide. Access is gained from a sloping walkway just west of a pull-in on the A381 Teignmouth to Newton Abbot road near Bishopsteignton. After going under the line and walking west on the shore line, a concrete 'Pill Box' is found and this offers some elevation for a picture of trains travelling in both directions. On 22 June 2008, the 10.57 Paddington to Plymouth travels adjacent to the River Teign near Bishopsteignton led by Class 43 No. 43018. **Author**

Above: *With the village of Bishopsteignton in the middle distance with a population of just over 2,500, Class 50 'Hoover' No. 50049* Defiance *approaches the footpath crossing of the line mid-way between Teignmouth and Newton Abbot on 7 July 1984. The train is the 07.40 Penzance to Glasgow, which the Class 50 operated as far as Birmingham New Street. The footpath from which this image was recorded also provides access to the foreshore which can offer further photographic opportunities of the line.* **Author**

Below: *Carrying BR green livery with a small yellow warning panel, North British Loco Co-built Class 43 'Warship' No. D850* Swift *pulls away from Newton Abbot towards Bishopsteignton in the late-1960s with a London-bound express. Note the tower of the long gone Newton Abbot power station on the left in the background and the yellow square carriage destination boards on the sides of the coaches, a feature of the Western Region in the 1970s.* **Peter Gray**

Above: The four tracks of Newton Abbot's Hackney yard, of which in 2008 only two were in use, are frequently used by Freightliner Heavy Haul to recess aggregate traffic en route *from and* to Cornwall. On 22 June 2008, Class 66/6 No. 66625 stands at the head of empty boxes awaiting departure the following morning as the 03.20 to Burngullow. **Kevin Wills**

Left: On the afternoon of 7 March 1997 the 15.35 Paddington to Penzance derailed as it approached the Newton Abbot station due to the collapse of a wheel bearing on TSO No. 42078, which landed straddling the centre beam of the bridge just east of the station. The entire was derailed, but thankfully nobody was seriously injured. This was the scene the following day while recovery operations were under way. **Author**

Below: Taken close to Newton Abbot East signal box, this period view of the station area records the transition between steam and diesel-hydraulic operation. Taken in September 1959 it shows the 'up' Devonian from Paignton to Leeds powered by GW 'Castle' No. 5055 Earl of Eldon *departing the station, while on the right is immaculate BR Swindon-built 'Warship' No. D806 Cambrian.* **D. Fish**

Newton Abbot

First Great Western

Top: *The present Newton Abbot station, rationalised in the mid-1980s when the West of England re-signalling was carried out, consists of just three reversable working platforms, principally an 'up' and 'down' main line and a 'loop', with the main station building in the background and cars parked on what was once a running lines. A First Great Western HST set awaits departure with the 07.43 Penzance to Paddington via Bristol on 23 June 2008 led by power car No. 43162. In the down main platform is a Class 142 set forming an Exmouth to Paignton service.* **Author**

Right Middle: *The present Newton Abbot station is a substantial structure opened on 11 April 1927 by Lord Mildmay of Flete. It was, and still is, a grand building, with booking office and information office on the ground floor and office accommodation on two floors above. Some modernisation was carried out in the 1990s to provide automatic sliding doors and improved passenger access. The building is officially known as South Devon House.* **Author**

Right Bottom: *Viewed from the road bridge crossing the line just to the west of Newton Abbot station, is this excellent vista of the station and depot. The long-closed up through line is on the left, followed by four platform faces down through line and the carriage sidings and depot tracks. Maroon with full yellow end liveried 'Western' No. D1016* Western Gladiator *heads west on 12 June 1969 forming the 08.50 Liverpool Lime Street to Plymouth service.* **L. Riley**

Left: *Compared with the view on the previous page, the vista from the road bridge west of Newton Abbot today reflects little of the golden past of the station and its surrounding area, with just three tracks, derelict buildings to the right and industrial units where the depot and works once stood. The train itself is of the 'modern' order, a Rail Head Treatment Train (RHTT) operated on behalf of Network Rail by Colas Rail to improve adhesion by keeping leaf mulch off the rails in the leaf fall season. Top and tailed by Nos. 47749 and 47727 and running as the 10.25 Par to Par via Newton Abbot, the train departs from platform 1 on 14 October 2007.* **Author**

Right: *Departing from Newton Abbot and passing under the road bridge at the west end of the station, a pair of North British Loco Co Type 2s, Nos. D6353 and D6301, head west on 18 July 1962. Some of the services at this time had loco exchanges or pilots added at Newton Abbot for the arduous climb of the Devon banks west of Newton Abbot.* **A. P. Crane**

Left: *Rail blue-liveried North British 'Warship' No. D852 Tenacious pulls away from Newton Abbot and heads towards Aller Junction on 27 July 1970 with the 11.20 Paddington to Penzance service formed of a rake of blue and grey-liveried Mk.1 coaches. At this time the Newton Abbot power station cooling tower was still in existence, as was the wonderful Great Western lower quadrant ring arm on the up relief track. By the time this illustration was taken, a new footbridge had been built adjacent to the road bridge.* **L. Riley**

ALLER AND THE PAIGNTON/PLYMOUTH SPLIT

Directly west of Newton Abbot is Aller Junction, which is the point at which trains to Torquay, Paignton and Kingswear branch off the main line via Dainton bank to Totnes, Plymouth and Cornwall.

Originally two single tracks were laid out of Newton Abbot and after one mile veered away from each other. The first physical junction was opened on 29 January 1855 when Torquay Junction opened, which came about as the two tracks west of Newton Abbot now both serviced the Plymouth line with a single line divergence to the Paignton and Kingswear route.

From 1874 a third track was laid from the junction to Newton Abbot station, which was used by Kingswear line services. Growth in traffic flows was such that a fourth line between Newton Abbot and Torquay Junction opened as part of the doubling of the Newton Abbot to Kingskerswell section of the Kingswear line.

At the time of plans to rebuild Newton Abbot station prior to World War I it was proposed to build a flying junction by the village of Aller, close to Torquay Junction which would allow high speed divergence and joining of trains from both lines. However the outbreak of hostilities saw this plan shelved and on 25 May 1925 a new junction was installed at Aller, known as Aller Junction. The layout of the tracks was complex and pairs of lines were grouped by direction. From right to left when looking at the layout from Aller - down Paignton, down Plymouth, up Paignton and up Plymouth. The junction layout at Aller allowed full interconnection between lines.

This arrangement was not welcomed by operators, for it required all 'up' Paignton line trains to cross over the 'down' Plymouth line, which caused serious delays at times of peak traffic, especially on summer Saturdays.

However, the arrangement remained until the West of England re-signalling which called for a much simpler junction layout. Just three tracks were provided west from Newton Abbot for around half a mile, where the Paignton route split into two tracks. The two twin-track routes then ran side by side to the point of the former Aller Junction before diverging to their respective destinations. At this time, April 1987, Aller Junction was officially renamed Aller Divergence and the lines of running right to left at the junction were renamed down Paignton, up Paignton, down Plymouth and up Plymouth. ∎

Above: *Crossing the complex junction layout at Aller, pulling off the 'up' Paignton line and crossing the 'down' Plymouth in the process, Class 50 No. 50009* Conqueror *powers a Paignton to Plymouth via Newton Abbot train. Aller Junction box, with its 46 levers is seen on the left.* **Author**

Below: *A view from Aller farm bridge looking east on 8 April 2002. On the left a Class 150/2 forms a Plymouth to Newton Abbot service, while the 13.33 Paddington to Plymouth, led by Class 43 power car No. 43186 heads west, overtaking Class 150/2 No. 150221 forming the 14.54 Exmouth to Paignton all stations service. The two down trains are approaching Aller divergence, while the physical junction is round the curve in the distance controlled by the two colour light signals.* **Author**

Above: *Taken from the position of Aller Junction signal box, this is the view looking east, towards Aller farm bridge. Taken on 29 May 2003, GBRf Class 66/7 No. 66717 takes the Plymouth line with the second portion of the Hope to Moorswater cement. Due to a shortage of Freightliner Heavy Haul traction the GBRf loco was on a short term hire to Freightliner and was the first ever GBRf Class 66 to work over the Sea Wall. Note 'The Bulkliner' headboard on the front.* **Author**

Below: *The Aller farm bridge looking west offers a perfect view of the physical divergence of the Paignton and Plymouth lines at what was once Aller Junction. On 20 July 2002, BR rail-blue Class 47 No. 47840 North Star pulls off the Paignton line forming the 16.17 Summer Saturday Paignton to Manchester Piccadilly formed of a hired-in Virgin West Coast Mk.3 passenger set including a DVT.* **Author**

Above: *The trial electric train heat (ETH) fitted Class 57/6, No. 57601, modified with funding from Porterbrook leasing using a refurbished Class 47 body and installing a second-hand refurbished General Motors 645 series engine and rebuilt by Brush Traction, was tested on Great Western services in advance of a squadron order for four locos being placed to power GW overnight sleeper services between Paddington and Penzance. On 19 June 2002, No. 57601, painted in Porterbrook silver and purple livery with stylised numbers, rounds Aller divergence off the Plymouth line with the 09.20 Plymouth to Paddington via Bristol service.* **Author**

Right: *A Virgin Cross Country 2+7 HST formation, led by power car No. 43184 heads towards Aller farm bridge and the line divergence on 8 April 2002 forming the 06.40 Dundee to Penzance. At the time this was the longest through rail journey in the UK. On the far right side is the main Exeter to Torbay road, the A380.* **Author**

Film Strip: 1. *The farm bridge at Aller is a very popular location with photographers when any unusual or steam powered trains are about. This large group of photographers was captured on 20 July 2002 waiting for 47840, illustrated left to pass.* **2**. *The unique Hornby-liveried Class 43 No. 43087 passes Aller on 13 February 2006 with a Bishops Lydeard to Laira stock move.* **3**. *Loadhaul liveried Class 60 No. 60007 approaches Aller on 16 July 2002 with the 08.58 Stoke to St Blazey.* **4**. *Green-liveried Class 47 No. 47851 passes Aller on 8 April 2002 with the 15.55 Plymouth to Sheffield. All:* **Author**

Above: *Just west of Aller Junction, on the Totnes and Plymouth route, a bridge known as Langford Bridge, crosses the line. Although today very busy with truck traffic, years ago it was a quiet country lane offering a nice location for an afternoon's photography. Until the early 1980s a down loop track existed between Aller Junction and Langford bridge which was frequently used by ballast trains working between Newton Abbot and Stoneycombe Quarry. Taking the main line, North British Type 2 diesel-hydraulic No. D6336 pilots BR-built GW-design 'Castle' 4-6-0 No. 7037* Swindon *(the last 'Castle' built) working the 05.30 Paddington to Penzance on 29 September 1961. The Type 2 had been added to pilot the train over the Devon banks as far as Plymouth.* **W. L. Underhay**

Below: *Without the down 'loop' track and with well-grown lineside vegetation, Virgin Trains-liveried Class 47 No. 47831* Bolton Wanderer *pulls round the curve at Aller and approaches Langford Bridge on 15 July 2002 forming the 06.05 Derby to Plymouth. This loco was later rebuilt as Class 57/3 No. 57310 for Virgin Trains West Coast 'Thunderbird' duties.* **Author**

Above: *Viewed from Langford Bridge looking west but showing an eastbound train, Police-liveried Class 47 No. 47829 slows on the descent of Dainton bank for the Aller curve on 13 April 2002 while powering the 08.42 Penzance to Manchester Piccadilly service. No. 47829 was repainted in Police livery and rolled out at Birmingham International on 25 March 2002 as part of an anti-trespass campaign.* **Author**

Right Middle: *Network Rail operated inspection saloon No. 975025, a converted Hastings line buffet car and the former Southern Region General Manager's saloon is still to be found on the National Network operating line of route inspections. Recently modified with blue star controls, the saloon previously operated using the older Southern Region EMU multiple control system and was powered by either Class 33/1s or 73s. On 16 March 2006, No. 975025 is seen propelled by Class 33/1 No. 33103 and heading towards Aller on the Paignton line forming the 09.35 Exeter St Davids to Penzance via Barnstaple, Paignton and Newquay.* **Author**

Right Bottom: *Directly west of Aller on the Paignton line is the Barn Owl Bridge, which takes its name from an adjacent public house. The bridge offers pleasing views of the Paignton branch in both directions. In the period when Virgin Trains hired EWS Class 67s to operate additional summer relief holiday trains to Paignton, No. 67021 approaches the Barn Owl Bridge powering the 07.08 York to Paignton formed of Virgin Trains Mk.2 stock on 31 July 2004. The Paignton branch is usually the domain of Class 142, 150, 153 and 159 DMUs, together with HST sets operating FGW London services and Arriva Cross Country Voyager stock working inter-regional services. The branch also sees some steam activity with charter services visiting the Paignton & Dartmouth Steam Railway.* **Author**

TRACK INSPECTION SERVICES

Track inspections of the entire UK rail network are very important to ensure the safe operation of the system. While most inspections are carried out on foot, several train-borne test vehicles are in operation. These are not a new feature to the network and were introduced in pre-Nationalisation days.

In 1928 the Great Western Railway Experimental Department at Swindon took over Collett third corridor brake No. 2360 and converted it into a track inspection or 'whitewash' coach, throwing out whitewash where track irregularities were found. The vehicle remained in traffic on the Western Region until 1989 as No. DW139.

Today, track inspection and recording is a very complex computer based operation involving highly sophisticated equipment mounted in the main on purpose built or converted vehicles. In terms of the Dawlish Sea Wall, the line sees frequent visits of the New Measurement Train (NMT), formed of modified Mk.3 stock powered by HST power cars. This usually operates on a Friday between Paddington and Plymouth and return, providing an immediate print out of track condition and irregularities.

From time to time when the HST power cars are not available, a pair of DRS-owned Class 37s power the measurement train vehicles.

In addition a two-car test DMU, based on the Class 150/1 design visits the area about three times every year, usually working west from its Derby base and visiting all main and branch lines.

Another interesting test train that occasionally traverses the Sea Wall is the Structure Gauging Train, formed of three ex-passenger vehicles and a purpose built laser coach. Usually operated at night, the vehicle 'fires' controlled lasers at lineside structures measuring they are at the correct distance from the tracks. ∎

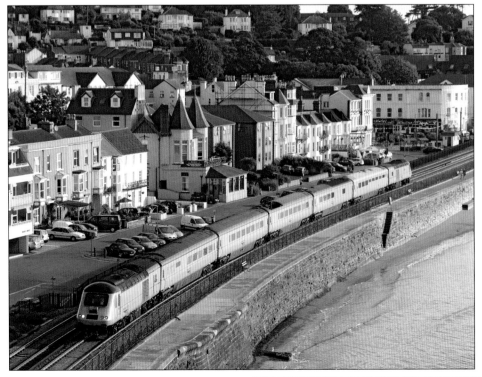

Top: *The old Great Western 'Whitewash' coach, No. DW139, remained in operation until the late 1980s and was a frequent visitor to the Sea Wall. Here on 17 March 1982 the coach is seen as the rear vehicle of a Swindon to Plymouth test formation powered by Class 47 No. 47509.* **Inset:** *Details of the coach with its unique angled side to ease observation. Both:* **Author**

Above: *High Speed Track Recording Coach No. DB999550, built to a modified Mk.2 specification, was introduced in 1973 and programmed to travel around 80,000 miles over the UK network coupled to service trains or as a departmental special. In its original guise the vehicle is seen at Dawlish Warren on 12 September 1980.* **Author**

Left: *The most significant development in track inspection and assessment in recent years has been the formation of the Network Rail New Measurement Train or NMT. Formed of Mk.3 stock powered by Class 43 HST power cars the set has a top speed of 125mph and operates to a timetabled schedule throughout the main lines of the UK. It visits the Dawlish Sea Wall on irregular Fridays working a return run from Paddington to Plymouth. It is seen passing Dawlish on 10 August 2007 formed with power cars Nos. 43062 and 43013.* **Author**

Above: 'Top and tailed' by Class 31s Nos. 31285 and 31106, the Structure Gauging Train crosses Cockwood Harbour on 27 March 2007 running as the 18.05 Exeter St Davids DMU Depot to Penzance. The actual laser test vehicle is coupled between the rear two passenger coaches. The ends of these coaches are painted black to stop unwanted reflection from the laser light. **Author**

Left: The Class 150/1 outline two-car recording unit visits the Dawlish Sea Wall about three times every year as part of a programmed operation to include all main and branch lines in the west. On 3 October 2006, set No. 950001 passes Dawlish forming the 08.30 Exeter St Davids DMU Depot to Penzance via Falmouth. **Author**

Right: Since its introduction, if the New Measurement Train (NMT) has been out of service a stand-in formation has been marshalled to perform the vital inspection role. This was the case on 15 September 2006 when DRS Class 37/6s Nos. 37607 and 37608 worked 'top and tail' of vehicles 6264, 977868, 999550, and 977986. The formation is seen passing along the Dawlish Sea Wall at Rockstone Bridge as train 1A94, the 10.15 Plymouth to London Paddington. **Author**

The Network Rail New Measurement Train (NMT) pulls slowly through Teignmouth on 10 August 2007 forming the Fridays only 1Z87 10.06 Plymouth to Paddington. The train is formed of power car No. 43062 John Armitt, saloons 977995, 975814, 977993, 977994, 975984 with power car No. 43013 on the rear. The third Mk.3 in the train is a pantograph test vehicle used for overhead line inspection and recording. **Author**